The BOURBON BARTENDER

The BOURBON BARTENDER

50 COCKTAILS to CELEBRATE the AMERICAN SPIRIT

JANE DANGER & ALLA LAPUSHCHIK

FOREWORD BY CLAY RISEN

PHOTOGRAPHY BY MAX KELLY

STERLING EPICURE

New York

STERLING EPICURE
New York

An Imprint of Sterling Publishing Co., Inc.
1166 Avenue of the Americas
New York, NY 10036

Some recipes in this book contain part of a raw egg. Consuming raw or undercooked eggs
may increase your risk of food-borne illness. The young, elderly, pregnant women, and
anyone who may be immune-compromised should not consume them.

ISBN 978-1-4549-2629-0

Distributed in Canada by Sterling Publishing Co., Inc.
c/o Canadian Manda Group, 664 Annette Street
Toronto, Ontario, Canada M6S 2C8
Distributed in the United Kingdom by GMC Distribution Services
Castle Place, 166 High Street, Lewes, East Sussex, England BN7 1XU
Distributed in Australia by NewSouth Books
45 Beach Street, Coogee, NSW 2034, Australia

For information about custom editions, special sales, and premium and
corporate purchases, please contact Sterling Special Sales
at 800-805-5489 or specialsales@sterlingpublishing.com.

Manufactured in Canada

2 4 6 8 10 9 7 5 3 1

sterlingpublishing.com

Interior design by Christine Heun
A complete list of image credits appears on p. 141.

To Natalie & Laurel,
the smart, strong, beautiful women
who made us and loved us

CONTENTS

FOREWORD

You can drink whiskey anywhere. Ernest Shackleton took 46 cases on his ill-fated trip to Antarctica. My grandfather took it in a flask to the golf course. I like it on a back porch late in the afternoon. But whiskey's natural habitat is the bar, and any bar will do: it's at home in the diviest of dive bars and the snootiest of private clubs. Order it neat, on the rocks, with soda, in a cocktail—anything goes. Whiskey is the white Oxford shirt or little black dress of the spirits world.

The book you're holding concerns itself with whiskey, bourbon in particular, cocktails specifically, and it couldn't come at a better time. Bourbon and cocktails have undergone an incredible renaissance in recent years, but what's been happening signifies so much more than that. We're not just going back to the old days and old ways of drinking. We're not just drinking bourbon the way our grandparents did. Craft distillers are producing exciting, innovative expressions—hopped whiskey, quinoa whiskey, port-finished bourbon—that are challenging and expanding the category itself. Bartenders are using those innovative creations to develop twists and turns on classic cocktails and completely new recipes that make today's bar scene the most exciting since Prohibition brought the last golden age of cocktails to a swift end.

Many of those recipes, old and new, call simply for whiskey, but they really mean bourbon—because not all whiskeys are the same. Scotch is a cat, finicky and refined; it doesn't play well with others. Scotch guards its secrets, demanding attention, contemplation, focus. You can find recipes for scotch cocktails, but beyond a few classics—Rob Roy, Rusty Nail—they appeal mostly to particular palates. Bourbon, in contrast, is a golden retriever. Enjoyable on its own, it plays equally well with others. Its robust sweetness and underlying bite support a body of invigorating spice, tangy citrus, and energizing bitterness. Its big, bold notes of vanilla, cinnamon, and stone fruits eagerly romp with other ingredients. It likes nothing more than to tumble into a glass with a few mixers. Bourbon cocktails are plentiful and plenty delicious.

That's no coincidence. Bourbon and cocktails grew up together. The first bourbons, as we know them today, arose in Kentucky around the turn of the nineteenth century before migrating to Ohio and, via the Mississippi River, down to New Orleans, where they first gained popularity in the 1820s. Distillers didn't age bourbon at first, but drinkers soon developed a taste for expressions that had sat for a few months or more in a barrel, losing some of the harsh bite, absorbing caramel and vanilla notes, and taking on a reddish-amber hue. Bourbon proper was born.

Not long afterward, travelers noted a new breed of bartenders mixing a new breed of drinks. Slings, Mint Juleps, and the like weren't meant to mask impurities in low-grade spirits; rather, they amplified the pleasant tastes emerging from this new generation of spirits. Jerry Thomas wrote the world's first bartender guide in 1862, right around the time that phylloxera, a grape louse, began decimating the vineyards of Europe. The wine economy suffered enormously, of course, but the Cognac industry plummeted as well. Ever-adaptable bartenders soon swapped brandy for whiskey in the Sazerac and other concoctions. The Old-Fashioned rose to prominence, as did the Manhattan, Boulevardier, and Saratoga. Over the next six decades, the American cocktail scene grew. Whiskey flourished alongside it.

Mixing drinks soon became an art. By the early twentieth century, bourbon stood behind the bar of establishments from low to high and from coast to coast, perfectly supporting a wide range of cocktails. When the vodka craze of the 1980s and 1990s finally waned, distillers and bartenders cast their gaze back on the brown stuff. Mixologists uncovered those forgotten classic recipes, rediscovering the joys of bourbon, and turned to the future with new mixtures, the highlights of which you'll find in these pages.

The news keeps getting better, too. Today's bartenders have more than just Jim Beam or Elijah Craig at their disposal. As of 2016, America has more than 500 whiskey distilleries, most making bourbon and each trying to make its mark with a unique, complex expression. Some have a high, spicy rye content; others finish in wine barrels; but all give bartenders a broad palette for creating the next generation of cocktails.

Cocktailing is an art: it's easy to learn, but it takes years to master. You don't have to be a mixologist to make these delicious drinks, but this book will set you on that splendid path. Jane and Alla stand at the forefront of the craft cocktail renaissance, and they write with verve on a subject dear to their hearts. Heed their expertise and you'll come away with insight, knowledge, and skill. Then, at the end of a long day, mix up a batch of bourbon drinks for you and your significant other or loved ones. Take pride in the accomplishment, then drink up and feel good. The task becomes its own reward.

Clay Risen

Eli Barnum & Benj. Brooks
Still

INTRODUCTION
A SHORT HISTORY OF BOURBON

From America's earliest beginnings, settlers came to these shores with a raging thirst. John Alden, a cooper, sailed aboard the *Mayflower* to tend to the ship's precious barrels. When he came to the New World, John Winthrop, governor of the Massachusetts Bay Colony, brought 10,000 gallons of beer, 120 hogsheads of malt for brewing, and 12 gallons of "hot waters," or ardent spirits. Even for the dour Puritans, drink was a gift from God. They expected no one to toil without refreshment.

By 1629 the Virginia Colony had two brewhouses. Boston established its first malt house in 1637. Willem Kieft, director general of the New Netherland Colony, was distilling grain—probably corn or rye—by 1640. But New World colonists had difficulty re-creating the drinks of the Old World. Climates differed, and the European ingredients weren't available. Colonists began fermenting whatever they had on hand to satisfy their thirst, including apples, bran, currants, elderberries, fir needles, hemlock, Jerusalem artichokes, parsnips, peaches, pears, pine buds, pine chips, roasted corn, and sassafras roots. Cider became especially popular. To concentrate cider, New Englanders put containers of it outdoors in cold weather, waited for it to freeze, and then skimmed off the ice. By 1668, William Laird, a Scottish distiller plying his trade in Monmouth County, New Jersey, was making apple brandy, thereby establishing one of America's oldest distilleries (known today as Laird & Company).

But rum reigned as king. New England— one of the corners of the lucrative molasses trade (slaves, sugar, rum)—boasted 159 rum distilleries in 1770. In smaller amounts, the colonists also made whiskey from rye. Then the War of Independence halted the triangular trade among America, Britain, and the Caribbean, changing the game. As the eighteenth century drew to a close, settlers continued moving inland and turned increasingly to corn, a native grain that held up better than rye, wheat, and other European species. The Whiskey Rebellion of 1791 bears witness to the

OPPOSITE Still design patented by Elijah Barnum and Benjamin Brooks of New Marlborough, Massachusetts, in 1808.

rising importance of American whiskey. On the western frontier of present-day Kentucky, settlers—including Jacob Beam, Basil Hayden, Robert Samuels, and Daniel Weller, all ancestors of future players in the bourbon world—brought their stills over the Appalachian Mountains.

Farmers had been converting surplus grain into alcohol for centuries (because before modern sanitation it proved safer to drink than water), but in the nineteenth century whiskey making became a vocation in its own right. Soon, alongside tobacco, Kentucky was exporting huge volumes of whiskey, which traveled downriver, taking on its unique characteristics, including the name.

After the Revolutionary War, Kentucky still was part of Virginia. Officials subdivided the district into smaller counties, giving French names to many of them in honor of America's wartime ally. Fayette County took its name from the marquis de la Fayette, and Bourbon County from the House of Bourbon, led by King Louis XVI of France, who helped finance the rebellion. In these counties, farmer-distillers were making corn whiskey and selling it as an easier way to make a profit than trying to haul corn around. Exports from Bourbon County, which then included a large swath of present-day Kentucky, traveled from the port town of Limestone—Maysville today—down the Ohio River to the Mississippi.

> **FUN FACT**
>
> The blue limestone in Kentucky and Tennessee purifies the water that runs through it, removing salt and adding calcium.

When Kentucky became a state in 1792, Bourbon County split up further. (It originally consisted of 34 modern-day counties.) Despite the new boundaries, people still called the

OPPOSITE Louis XVI, king of France, head of the House of Bourbon, and namesake of Bourbon County, Kentucky. ABOVE Maysville, Kentucky, on the Ohio River.

TOP Angered by a 1791 federal tax on whiskey that effectively eliminated their profits, farmers in Pennsylvania both threatened and attacked excise agents.
BOTTOM George Washington, Alexander Hamilton, and others lead federal troops to suppress the Whiskey Rebellion.

Workers at Labrot & Graham's Old Oscar Pepper Distillery, today the Woodford Reserve Distillery, in Versailles, Kentucky.

entire region Old Bourbon, and any of the corn whiskey traveling down from Limestone was called Old Bourbon Whiskey. Drinkers on the receiving end developed a taste for the spirit and began asking for it by name. Many of those drinkers lived in New Orleans, which still was part of the French Empire, and noted the similarities between this corn whiskey and their beloved Cognac. Corn distillers, spotting a good marketing opportunity, adopted the name for their corn whiskey no matter where it was made.

Like converting surplus grain into alcohol, the tradition of aging beer, wine, and spirits in wooden barrels stretches far into the past. Brewers, vintners, and distillers all know that wood aging can increase complexity, but bourbon was selling just fine unaged, or "green." By 1814, though, some expressions included age statements. Merchants used barrels to store and transport just about everything, so between uses they often charred the interiors to prevent fishy whiskey and other accidental cross-contamination.

With the advent and improvement of the column still in the 1820s and 1830s, capacity increased. As a result, many distillers set aside extra product to avoid flooding the market and driving prices down, but longer storage times pulled barrels from the standard rotation among goods. Cooperages had to make new barrels. Around this time it probably became standard for distillers to age bourbon in new, charred barrels.

Although the consumption of bourbon has varied over time, the methods of making it have remained relatively unchanged for nearly two centuries, but bourbon traveled a long path from the early days of frontier distilling to official status as America's national spirit. That distinction happened on May 4, 1964. On that date, Congress jointly passed concurrent legislation that US Senator Thurston Morton from Louisville and US Representative John C. Watts from Nicholasville had introduced. Congress established bourbon as a "distinctive product of the United States" and defined its legal parameters.

OPPOSITE J. H. Cutter whiskey barrels.

LEGAL DEFINITIONS

WHISKEY

Spirits distilled from a fermented mash of grain at less than 95 percent alcohol by volume (190 proof) having the taste, aroma, and characteristics generally attributed to whiskey and bottled at not less than 40 percent alcohol by volume (80 proof).

BOURBON

Whiskey produced in the U.S. at not exceeding 80 percent alcohol by volume (160 proof) from a fermented mash of not less than 51 percent corn and stored at not more than 62.5 percent alcohol by volume (125 proof) in charred new oak containers.

STRAIGHT BOURBON WHISKEY

Bourbon whiskey stored in charred new oak containers for two years or more. It may include mixtures of two or more straight bourbon whiskeys provided all of the whiskeys are produced in the same state.
(Alcohol and Tobacco Tax and Trade Bureau)

Making bourbon represents a labor of love for a select few. For the rest of us, the fun begins when we use it to make drinks for all occasions. Let's explore the quintessential American spirit and its delicious role in timeless classics, forgotten gems, and craft concoctions.

TOOLS & TECHNIQUES

BARWARE

BARSPOONS

Barspoons usually come in two types: one for style and grace and one for utility. The first often has a teardrop, tongue, or weight at the top to help you stir in a mixing glass. The utility spoon usually has a red tip and larger round bowl for cracking or shaping ice.

BLENDER

Use a stick or immersion blender for soft or liquid ingredients and a countertop model for ice.

JIGGER

Cover all bases with a 1-ounce and a 2-ounce jigger and a ½-ounce and a ¾-ounce jigger. Accuracy matters.

JUICER

Fresh juice is absolutely essential for good cocktails, so invest in a good electric or handheld model.

MIXING GLASS

Glass preserves the temperature of a drink better than the metal of a shaking tin, and you can keep an eye on what's happening inside. Use a pint glass in a pinch.

MUDDLER

This truncheon releases the flavor of herbs and fruit and doubles as a bludgeon. Wooden ones require maintenance, and textured ones can mash delicate ingredients. Go for one that's smooth and heavy.

SHAKERS

Various styles include the Parisian (two stainless steel tins that join with a clean seam), the cobbler (cap over strainer, which fits into the bottom tin), and the Boston (pint glass plus large shaking tin). We prefer the weighted shaker, in which a smaller metal shaker fits into a larger shaker, typically 18 and 28 ounces, respectively. You'll see this behind the bar most often.

SPEED POURERS

These allow you to measure accurately without spilling by controlling the flow of liquid from the bottle. Make sure the speed pourer forms a proper seal with the bottle to prevent mess and waste.

STRAINERS

The Hawthorne strainer has a flat top, a central perforation, and a metal spiral around the edge. It fits snugly into the large tin of any shaker, and pushing the spiral forward allows you to adjust the strain. Julep strainers consist of a shallow perforated bowl on a handle and should fit snugly into your mixing glass to strain stirred drinks.

Y-SHAPED VEGETABLE PEELER

This design gives you more control than a straight vegetable peeler for making proper twists.

GLASSWARE

BEER STEIN OR GLASS
This pint glass (16 ounces) can be cylindrical with a handle, conical, or nonik ("no-nick"), which bulges slightly toward the top.

COLLINS GLASS
This tall, cylindrical glass, named after the Tom Collins cocktail, holds 10 to 14 ounces and helps preserve carbonation.

COPPER MUG
These handled metallic cups are the proper serving vessels for bucks and mules.

COUPE
This timeless classic holds 5 to 6 ounces. Reportedly modeled after Marie Antoinette's left breast and formerly used for sparkling wine, it's now the bartender's choice for craft cocktails.

HIGHBALL
This 8-ounce hybrid of the Collins and rocks glasses perfectly accommodates drinks with two parts still liquids to one part sparkling. The name comes from a piece of railroad equipment and originally indicated how quickly the drink could be made.

IRISH COFFEE MUG

This handled ceramic cup or glass holds 6 to 8 ounces. Glass versions are narrower to avoid heat loss.

JULEP CUP

This conical, footed silver cup features either a banded or a beaded rim. This Kentucky tradition dates back to the early 1800s.

ROCKS GLASS

Usually as tall as they are wide, standard versions hold 6 to 7 ounces, perfect for a 2-ounce pour over a handful of ice cubes. Larger versions can handle 10 ounces or more, providing enough room for a strong cocktail and big ice.

SHOT GLASS

Small glasses of varying shapes and styles that typically hold 1.5 ounces.

WINEGLASS

Copious permutations of this stemmed and footed glass bowl that holds 4 to 8 ounces accommodate different kinds and styles of wine, but you can use it for cocktails as well.

INGREDIENTS

BITTERS

These erstwhile medicinal concoctions now balance and cut the sweetness of cocktails. Flavors vary widely, so when we specify a particular brand, we mean it.

BOURBON

Again, when we specify a particular brand, we mean it. Bourbon offers a diversity of nuances that play well in cocktails, providing nearly endless flavor options. Mash bill, age, blend, proof—all combine to make individual expressions with unique character. In the recipes that follow, we indicate our favorite expressions or brands for what we consider the best flavor results, but feel free to try different kinds and see how they work to your taste.

CARBONATION

Bubbles come in many forms: club soda, ginger beer, seltzer, sparkling wine, and more. Always add carbonated ingredients after you've poured the drink into the serving glass. No shaking or mixing afterward!

CITRUS

Don't even think about store-bought bottles of juice or, worse, plastic squeeze containers of flavored water. Nothing beats the real thing. Always squeeze it fresh.

EGGS

Use small, organic eggs, rinse the shells thoroughly in cold water, coddle them quickly in 90–120°F water, and then dry them immediately. Note: consuming raw or undercooked eggs may increase your risk of food-borne illness.

GARNISHES

Always use the freshest fruits and herbs available. Mint, for example, wilts quickly at room temperature. Cherries for garnish should be brandied, such as the Luxardo brand. No neon red monsters!

ICE

Good, solid ice helps achieve a proper diluted, chilled, and balanced cocktail. Making your own may sound time consuming, but the payoff is worth it, and kitchen goods stores have a plethora of molds and trays from which to choose. If you don't have easy access to crushed ice, put a handful of ice cubes in a clean plastic bag and crush them with a muddler, mallet, or tenderizer before putting them into the cocktail shaker.

When you are serving a drink on the rocks, always build the complete drink and add the ice last, immediately before serving.

SYRUPS

These sugar solutions aren't just cloying sweeteners meant to ease or hide the bite of strong booze. They also add necessary body and flavor to cocktails and can temper stronger ingredients. See page 16 for recipes.

VERMOUTH

This wine fortified with neutral grape brandy comes in two main styles: dry (French) and sweet (Italian). See "The Rise of Vermouth" (page 28) for more.

SYRUPS

CHOCOLATE SYRUP

2 cups water
2 cups white sugar
2 ounces Dutch-process cocoa powder
2 cinnamon sticks
  zest of 1 orange

In a small pan, stir all the ingredients to combine. Simmer on low for about 10 minutes or until the syrup sticks to the back of a spoon. Strain. Keeps in the refrigerator for two weeks.

CINNAMON SYRUP

2 cups water
2 cups white sugar
10 cinnamon sticks

Combine all the ingredients in a saucepan, bring to a boil, and turn off the heat. Cover and let sit at room temperature for 24 hours. Strain out the cinnamon and refrigerate. Keeps in the refrigerator for two weeks.

CORN PUREE

1 can (15 ounces) sweet corn
1¼ cups white sugar

In a small pan, heat on low for 5 minutes or until the sugar dissolves. Puree. Keeps in the refrigerator for two weeks

DEMERARA SYRUP

2 cups water
2 cups demerara sugar

Heat in a saucepan on medium heat until sugar and water fully combine. Keeps in the refrigerator for two weeks.

GINGER SYRUP

1 cup ginger juice
1 cup demerara or brown sugar
1 cup white sugar

Combine in a saucepan and heat on low until sugar dissolves. Let cool and refrigerate. Keeps for two weeks.

GRENADINE

2 cups pomegranate juice
1 cup white sugar
⅛ teaspoon rose water
  peel of 1 large orange

Cook all ingredients over medium heat for 10 minutes. Strain out peel. Keeps in the refrigerator for two or three weeks.

HONEY SYRUP

1½ cups honey

1½ cups water

Heat on low until the ingredients combine. Keeps in the refrigerator for three weeks.

ORGEAT

1 pound whole raw almonds

4 cups water

2 cups white sugar

1 cup demerara or light brown sugar

1 ounce Cognac

¾ teaspoon orange flower water

Preheat oven to 350°F. In a food processor, grind the almonds medium to fine. Spread them on a baking sheet and cook for 12 to 15 minutes, until golden. In a deep pan, combine water, toasted almonds, and both sugars. Cook on medium heat until the mixture comes to a boil. Remove from heat and blend into a thick paste. Fine strain through cheesecloth or a fine wire-mesh strainer. Add the Cognac and orange flower water and stir well. Keeps in the refrigerator for two weeks.

PASSION FRUIT SYRUP

2 cups passion fruit puree

2 cups white sugar

Combine in a saucepan and cook on low heat, stirring until the sugar dissolves. Remove from heat and let cool. Keeps in the refrigerator for two weeks.

ROSE SYRUP

4 ounces dried edible roses

2 cups water

2 cups white sugar

Steep roses in warm water until the water becomes dark pink. Strain out the roses. Combine rose water and sugar in a small pan and bring to a boil. Simmer on low for 10 minutes. Remove from heat and let cool. Keeps in the refrigerator for two weeks.

SIMPLE SYRUP

2 cups water

2 cups white sugar

Stir in a pan on low heat until the ingredients combine. Keeps in the refrigerator for three weeks.

METHODS

BLEND

For a countertop blender and cubed or crushed ice, pulse generously to break the ice without breaking the machine. For a stick blender, always keep the blades and their protective cover below the surface level of the liquid. Otherwise you'll be wearing your cocktail rather than drinking it.

CHILL

Put glassware in a freezer for 10 minutes or fill it with an ice-water bath before mixing a drink. For hot drinks, do the opposite: chafe the glassware with hot water first.

GARNISH

For twists, hold the citrus with a kitchen towel and use a Y-shaped peeler, making sure to avoid the pith. Pinch the twist skin side down over the drink, rub it around the rim of the glass, and then float it skin side up in the drink. Always rasp cinnamon, nutmeg, and other grated garnishes fresh to optimize their aromatics.

MIX

Recipe conventions list alcohols first, then nonalcohols, and then both in descending volumes, but that's just for planning purposes. In building drinks to be shaken or stirred, start with the smaller-volume and least expensive ingredients first: dashes of bitters, fruits or herbs to be muddled, juices, syrups, modifiers, and finally the base spirit.

MUDDLE

You want to press rather than smash to coax the juices or oils from fruit or herbs. Crushing them will release bitterness from the plant structure rather than the botanical essence. When muddling mint, use only the leaves—no stems—and reserve the best sprig tops for garnish. Tap the mint against the back of your hand to release the oils before garnishing.

RIM

For a basic salt or sugar rim, wipe a lemon or lime wedge around the outside edge of the mouth of the glass. For heavier rims, such as rough sugar or citrus zest, use simple syrup in a small dish. Hold the glass upside down and roll the outside only in the rimming material. Use kosher rough salt and fine-textured (not powdered) sugar for rimming. Don't get any inside the glass or you'll radically alter the flavor of the drink.

SHAKE

Do it like you mean it—hard and fast—but don't go crazy: no more than 10 to 20 seconds. Shaking for too long will bruise (overdilute) the drink. You want to chill, dilute, and aerate the cocktail, not kill it. Always make sure the tin is sealed tightly and the tins align vertically on one side. Dry shaking uses no ice, and whip shaking uses only one cube or a few pellets of crushed ice. In making cocktails with eggs or cream, add them last to avoid curdling, and dry shake (see above) for 5 to 10 seconds to emulsify. Then shake with ice for 10 to 15 seconds to chill and dilute. Strain shaken drinks from the larger tin with a Hawthorne strainer.

STIR

Prepare stirred cocktails in a mixing glass with plenty of ice, which will dilute and chill them properly. Crack the ice so that you can fit more in the glass. Strain stirred drinks from the mixing glass through a Julep strainer into the serving glass.

STRAIN

Use a Hawthorne strainer for shaken drinks that contain fine pieces of ice that need to be removed, a Julep strainer for stirred drinks, and a fine strainer for drinks shaken with muddled ingredients or egg.

TEST

To check the temperature, use the back of your hand, checking from base to top. When you are stirring a cocktail, straw-test after 10 seconds or use the back of your hand, Japanese-style, if you are among friends. With practice, you'll learn how much more ice to add to control temperature and dilution.

INVENTING
THE
COCKTAIL

"The greatest of all contributions of the American way of life to the salvation of humanity."

–H. L. Mencken

Where did the cocktail originate? The physical process of making a mixed drink arose in Colonial taverns, which rivaled churches as social institutions in God-fearing America. Those establishments lay at the heart of the revolution but also caused a spirited disruption in the way people consumed alcohol. To keep drinkers in their cups longer, tavern keepers knew they had to keep them entertained. One tavern advertised that it had a "a beautiful MOOSE" that patrons could view. When large mammals didn't do the trick, proprietors set their sights on the refreshments: Calibogus, Cherry Bounce, Cider Royal, Flip, grog, mead, punch, Sangaree, sling, syllabub, and many more drinks that predate the rise of the cocktail.

The etymology of the word itself, like so much of drinking history, remains hard to pin down but easy to enjoy. *The Morning Post and Gazetteer*, a London newspaper, reported in 1798 that in a stroke of great fortune, the owner of a Downing Street tavern had won the lottery. He consequently erased the tabs of his bar patrons. Several days later, the paper ran a satirical article detailing which members of the government had tabs at the tavern and what their tabs contained. Prime Minister William Pitt the Younger owed for a "cock-tail (vulgarly called ginger)." The satire here lies in knowing that

PREVIOUS PAGES Men at the Hannah and Hogg bar, Chicago, 1889.

"cock-tail" was the vulgar word. At that time, breeders docked the tails of horses to indicate their status as mixed breeds, or cocktails. Mixed-breed horse, mixed drink—but what of the ginger? Because horses with perky tails commanded higher prices, breeders sometimes employed a tactic called gingering. Inserting a piece of ginger into the rear end of a horse gives it a perky tail. Drinking the first cocktails no doubt produced a similar eyes-wide-open, tail-held-high effect. *The Farmer's Cabinet*, a Vermont newspaper, claimed in 1803

that "a glass of cocktail" was "excellent for the head."

Then, in 1806, the definitive instance of the cocktail as a mixed alcoholic drink emerged. Editor Harry Croswell described it in *The Balance and Columbian Repository* of Hudson, New York, as "a stimulating liquor, composed of spirits of any kind, sugar, water, and bitters—it is vulgarly called *bittered sling*." The cocktail soon became an inherently American concept. What grows together goes together, so let's pair it with the American spirit, bourbon, and see what happens.

OLD-FASHIONED

The original cocktail possesses a timeless, elegant simplicity. You can make an Old-Fashioned in a variety of ways, but the template remains the same: spirit, sugar, water, bitters. In addition to the freedom to use any spirit you like—brandy, gin, rum, tequila, vodka, whiskey—there are different ways to handle the fruit and sugar in the recipe. In the 1930s, people began bludgeoning the fruit to death. Perhaps that masked the low quality of Prohibition-era spirits. Maybe Prohibition itself interrupted and undermined the craft of mixing a good drink and people simply forgot how to do it properly. Either way, in a 1936 letter to the *New York Times*, an irritated drinker described the contemporary bartenders' method of mixing an Old-Fashioned as well as its price of 30 cents as a "profanation and extortion." So unless you're drinking rotgut, don't slaughter an orchard of cherries and oranges to make your drink. Also, some people prefer to muddle a sugar cube, whereas others prefer the more delicate smoothness of simple syrup. Here's how to do it.

ROCKS

2 ounces Four Roses Small Batch bourbon

¼ ounce simple syrup (page 17)

3 dashes Angostura bitters

3 dashes Regans' orange bitters

orange and lemon for garnish

Stir all the liquid ingredients in a mixing glass filled with ice for 15 seconds and then strain into a rocks glass with ice. Garnish with an orange twist and a lemon twist.

VARIATION

If you prefer the texture of a sugar cube in your drink, substitute a demerara sugar cube for the simple syrup. Add the cube to the rocks glass, soak with bitters, and muddle. Add bourbon and ice and stir. Garnish as above.

SLING

This single-serving drink predates the cocktail proper and probably stems from punch, originally a batched five-ingredient mixture (spirit, sugar, water, fruit juice, spice) that made its way to England from India—where it was called *panch*, the Hindi word for "five"—in the early 1600s. First Lord of the Admiralty Edward Russell, earl of Orford, famously threw a party in 1694 in Cádiz, Spain, at which he served 750 gallons of punch on which a small boy floated in a boat, serving it to the guests. But let's reduce the scale a bit. At its most basic, a sling consists of spirit, sugar, and water. The addition of bitters transformed it into a Bittered Sling, which eventually became the cocktail, as noted by Harry Croswell (page 23). In the 1800s, bartenders were adding lemon juice to the mix, then Cherry Heering. If drinking historically interests you, give it a shot. Then add some bitters. Here's the 1941 *Mr. Boston* recipe.

ROCKS

2 ounces bourbon
1 teaspoon water
1 teaspoon powdered sugar

Build in a rocks glass, add ice, and stir.

MANHATTAN

The introduction of vermouth to the whiskey cocktail in the late nineteenth century revolutionized the art of mixing drinks and catalyzed cocktail culture as we know it today. But not all vermouths are created equal. Each has its own flavor profile and purpose (page 28). We prefer Carpano Antica, which adds a nice vanilla depth, and Dolin Rouge, which tastes lighter and fruitier. Depending on which you use, you can adjust the base spirit. Vermouth is fortified wine, which makes it susceptible to oxidation and spoilage. After you open a bottle, store it in the refrigerator and finish it or discard it after two months. Here are two versions, depending on which style you prefer.

DRY

COUPE

2 ounces Evan Williams bourbon

1 ounce Carpano Antica Formula dry vermouth

2 dashes Angostura bitters

cocktail cherry for garnish

SWEET

COUPE

2 ounces Rittenhouse bourbon

1 ounce Dolin Rouge sweet vermouth

2 dashes Angostura bitters

cocktail cherry for garnish

Stir all the ingredients in a mixing glass filled with ice and then strain into a chilled coupe. Garnish with cherry.

VARIATION

For a **PERFECT MANHATTAN**,
use ½ ounce each of sweet and dry vermouth.

THE RISE OF VERMOUTH

You've probably seen a bottle of vermouth left on a bar or counter for months, years even, waiting patiently but long past the prime of its deliciousness. It has left a bad taste in the collective mouth of the drinking public, sometimes literally, because of low-quality production or storage-induced spoilage. If you have an old bottle hanging around, crack open a fresh one and taste them side by side. You'll instantly understand the importance of following best storage practices.

Vermouth rose to national popularity in the 1860s first on its own as a medicinal apéritif and then in the 1880s as a constituent of mixed drinks. It stands at the heart of two of the most essential cocktails: the Manhattan (page 27) and the Martini. Over the course of the twentieth century, the Martini lost its vermouth altogether and deteriorated into a glass-based category, but that's a story for another book. The Manhattan, though, retained its vermouth—whether dry, sweet, or split—and its identity.

In 1953, Count Theo Rossi di Montelera, head of Martini & Rossi, inspected the American spirits market, convinced that tastes soon would change from expensive whiskey to vermouth. Tastes did change but not in vermouth's favor, and by the 1970s baby boomers viewed it with suspicion. At one point, the Harvard Club in Manhattan changed its Martini recipe from a ratio of 8:1 spirit to vermouth to 2:1. Alums voiced their crimson outrage, and the club reinstated the former spec. Vermouth slowly receded in the cocktail world, left sitting on the proverbial shelf, becoming undrinkable, and alienating a generation of drinkers. But with the bourbon renaissance, which began shortly after the turn of the new millennium, and education about proper storing, its star is rising again.

All vermouth derives from a white wine base. Any coloring results from flavor infusions, and it comes in a number of styles:

CHAMBÉRY BLANC The French producer Dolin popularized this colorless sweet style that tastes more herb-centric and less spicy than the Torino style. Example: Dolin Blanc.

CHAMBÉRY DRY France's Chambéry region developed a dry vermouth that avoided the oxidized flavors of the Marseilles style. It enjoyed popularity in America in the mid-twentieth century. Marseilles producers then produced extra-dry versions, made exclusively for the American market, to compete with this style. Example: Dolin Dry.

MARSEILLES DRY In the early nineteenth century, Provence developed its own style of vermouth for both drinking and cooking. Only one brand remains: Noilly Prat Original French Dry.

VERMOUTH ALLA VANIGLIA A favorite behind the bar, this is Torino with vanilla flavoring, which makes it work well with bourbon and other whiskeys. Example: Carpano Antica Formula.

VERMOUTH BIANCO In the early 1900s, vermouth brands were looking to diversify their export portfolios. This style took inspiration from Chambéry Blanc but tastes bolder with stronger vanilla notes. Examples: Carpano Bianco, Cinzano Bianco, Contratto Bianco.

VERMOUTH CHINATO These vermouths have added cinchona, a group of flowers from which quinine is extracted. Examples: Cocchi "Dopo Teatro" and Martini Gran Lusso.

VERMOUTH CON BITTER Basically Torino with added bitters, such as gentian. Example: Carpano Punt e Mes.

VERMOUTH TORINO Vermouth di Torino is a designation of controlled origin (DOC), like bourbon and Champagne, but the industry doesn't enforce it because few brands would meet the legal requirements. Examples: Carpano Classico, Cocchi Vermouth di Torino, Contratto Vermouth Rosso, Martini & Rossi Rosso.

WESTERN DRY This category encompasses contemporary American vermouth. After Prohibition, West Coast wine producers started producing vermouth again around 1998 as the cocktail renaissance blossomed. Examples: Vya and Imbue.

IMPROVED WHISKEY COCKTAIL

In the early days, the cocktail world was small and names didn't matter much, so for the first set of modifications or revisions the cocktails usually bore the name "Improved." Jerry Thomas, who made history with the first cocktail recipe book in 1862 (page 32), included an appendix of "improved" cocktails in his guide, and the improvements often consisted of adding absinthe or maraschino, an Italian liqueur made from Marasca cherries. The arrival of maraschino liqueur and its popularity coincided with the golden age of cocktails as well as the biggest influx of Italian immigrants, between 1880 and 1920, when 4 million people mostly from southern Italy came to America. Maraschino, which has essential pride of place in classics such as the Aviation, Last Word, and Martinez, became so important to a bartender's repertoire that Charles Baker wrote in his legendary *Gentleman's Companion* (1939) that "no fairly equipped bar can afford to be without it."

ROCKS

2 ounces Medley Brothers or Old Grand Dad 114 bourbon

¼ ounce maraschino liqueur

8 drops absinthe

2 dashes Angostura bitters

lemon for garnish

Stir in a mixing glass filled with ice and then strain into a rocks glass filled with ice. If you don't have a dropper for the absinthe, rinse the glass with a dash of it. Garnish with a lemon twist.

FUN FACT

An entire book on one brand of maraschino liqueur appeared in 1952: *Maraschino Luxardo: Evolution and History of a Famous Italian Liqueur* by Nicolo Luxardo de Franchi.

JERRY THOMAS

History remembers Jerry Thomas as the father of mixology. He wrote the first cocktail guide, *Bar-Tender's Guide, or How to Mix Drinks,* which Dick & Fitzgerald published in 1862. Before this watershed moment, bartenders shared their knowledge only verbally. He importantly categorized cocktails into families according to style for the first time, for example, the Brandy Daisy or Sour, which morphed into the Margarita or Daiquirí.

In addition to making history, Thomas had style and panache. He bejeweled not only himself but his sterling silver bar tools. Nor did the flash and pizzazz end there. His signature drink was the Blue Blazer: scotch, sugar, lemon peel, hot water, and *fire.* When the contents were lit ablaze, he tossed the drink back and forth between two silver mugs, making it the world's first flaming cocktail. As the man himself put it:

> The "blue blazer" does not have a very euphonious or classic name, but it tastes better to the palate than it sounds to the ear. A beholder gazing for the first time upon an experienced artist, compounding

this beverage, would naturally come to the conclusion that it was a nectar for Pluto rather than Bacchus. The novice in mixing this beverage should be careful not to scald himself. To become proficient in throwing the liquid from one mug to the other, it will be necessary to practise for some time with cold water.

Obviously lighting alcohol on fire and then tossing it around isn't safe. If you're in the mood for something hot, make a toddy instead (page 51).

After his death in 1885, the *New York Times* ran an obituary that read: "Jerry P. Thomas, one of the best known of the barkeepers of this city, died in his residence, Sixty-third-street and Ninth-avenue, on Monday afternoon of apoplexy. Soon after noon he left the Hotel Brighton for his home, and within five minutes after reaching it he dropped to the floor dead. He leaves a widow and two children." The Gray Lady didn't give him the most eloquent send-off, but Thomas still looms large as the man who started it all.

BLUE BLAZER.

SARATOGA

Jerry Thomas included this cocktail in his 1887 guide, where it appeared in print for the first time. It formed part of a family of drinks named for Saratoga Springs, New York, where the wealthy liked to bet on the ponies. Drink recipes that feature ingredients in equal parts exhibit a pleasing harmony both on the page and in the glass. Think of them as a measure of cocktail perfection and always pay close attention to the quality and type of each component. This cocktail tastes as sweet as victory at the races.

COUPE

1 ounce Redemption High Rye bourbon

1 ounce brandy

1 ounce sweet vermouth

2 dashes Angostura bitters

   lemon for garnish

Stir all the ingredients in a mixing glass filled with ice and then strain into a chilled coupe. Garnish with a lemon twist.

SUBURBAN COCKTAIL

The British-born James Keene made his money in mining, became president of the San Francisco Stock Exchange, lost his fortune, then made it again on Wall Street, and used it to feed his lifelong passion for horse racing. Ballot, one of his horses, won the Suburban Handicap race at Belmont Park in Elmont, New York, in 1908. According to Albert Stevens Crockett, author of *The Old Waldorf-Astoria Bar Book* (1935), this drink celebrated the triumphs of Keene "and his racing cohorts and other famous stable-owners on nearby courses." The cocktail remains interesting for its unusual yet delicious combination of spirits, all full of deep rich notes.

COUPE

1½ ounces bourbon

½ ounce dark rum

½ ounce Port

1 dash Angostura bitters

1 dash orange bitters

Stir all the ingredients in a mixing glass filled with ice and then strain into a chilled coupe.

TIP

The younger, fruiter notes of Ruby Port complement
this recipe, but also try it with the nuttiness of an older
Tawny Port, which works nicely with the rum and whiskey.

JULEP

The most southern of all beverages has a well-documented history. When Londoner John Davis was traveling America in 1803, he wrote that the Julep was "a dram of spirituous liquor that has mint steeped in it, taken by Virginians of a morning." The word derives, through Spanish, from the Persian word *golâb*, which means "rose water." Like the Old-Fashioned, early recipes and variations called for different spirits, including peach brandy and gin, in the service of settling a troubled stomach. The drink instantly communicated wealth and social status then as now, because it required access to ice, a rare commodity in the South then; a silver serving vessel; and of course a servant or slave to prepare and deliver it. In 1882, the Gage, Hittenger ice company schemed to create a taste for ice among Londoners by introducing them to the Mint Julep. Four years later, however, a *New York Times* reader wondered whether the Mint Julep had fallen from fashion. The popularity of the drink might have declined, if not in the 1880s, then certainly several decades later during Prohibition, but it remained novelist William Faulkner's favorite drink. Its association with the Kentucky Derby at Churchill Downs in Louisville dates to 1938. Today it stands proudly as the official cocktail of that event, with Woodford Reserve as the official brand.

JULEP CUP

10 mint leaves

2 ounces Woodford Reserve bourbon

½ ounce demerara syrup (page 16)

mint sprigs for garnish

Press the mint leaves around the inside of the cup. Add the liquid ingredients and crushed ice. Stir vigorously or swizzle with a barspoon until a frost develops around the outside of the cup. Garnish with mint sprigs and serve with a straw.

 The Mint Julep is one of mankind's truly civilized inventions.

–Charles H. Baker

WHISKEY SOUR

Like so many whiskey-based cocktails, this one suffered simplification and bastardization for the sake of convenience in the middle of the twentieth century. With beautifully simple cocktails like this, maintaining the caliber of the ingredients becomes even more important. In other words, ditch the sour mix, chip ice, and neon cherry monsters and give the Sour another chance. Its unexpected delicacy will surprise you. To entice you, we've given you not one but *three* versions of the drink, so you have no excuse not to give it a try.

ROCKS

2 ounces Old Forester bourbon
½ ounce demerara syrup (page 16)
¾ ounce lemon juice
½ ounce orange juice
orange and cocktail cherry for garnish

Shake with ice and double strain into a rocks glass filled with ice. Garnish with an orange wheel and cherry.

COUPE

2 ounces W. L. Weller Special Reserve bourbon
¾ ounce demerara syrup (page 16)
¾ ounce lemon juice
lemon for garnish

Shake with ice and double strain into a chilled coupe. Garnish with a lemon wheel.

VARIATION

For a SILVER WHISKEY SOUR, add 1 egg white to the second recipe above, which will give the cocktail a delicious frothy texture. Dry shake all ingredients and then shake again with ice. Strain into a chilled coupe.

NEW YORK SOUR

Eminent cocktail historian David Wondrich notes in *Imbibe!* that this drink went by the names Southern Whiskey Sour and Continental Sour during the 1880s, but the New York name stuck by the early 1900s. Make this one the next time you want to impress someone. Through the scientific magic of density, the wine floats on top of the sour in an aesthetically pleasing band of color.

ROCKS

1½ ounces Pure Kentucky bourbon
¾ ounce simple syrup (page 17)
¾ ounce lemon juice
dry red wine

Shake the first three ingredients with ice and double strain into a rocks glass filled with ice. Float the dry red wine to fill.

TIP

The secret to achieving the red wine float is easy: place a barspoon upside down over the surface of the sour mixture and against the side of the glass. Then gently pour the wine over the back of the spoon.

COLONEL COLLINS

The Collins family of drinks, like today's generic Martinis, forms around the glassware in which it's served. (A wide surface area allows too many of the bubbles to escape too quickly, so the slender Collins glass gives them less surface area from which to escape.) The paterfamilias John Collins combines gin, lemon, sugar, and club soda, and it may have originated with a bartender by that name who worked at Limmer's Old House in the Mayfair district of London, a popular destination for gin punch. As the recipe evolved in the nineteenth century, it called specifically for Old Tom gin, sweeter than the London Dry style, and took on a new name, the Tom Collins, possibly as a result of the infamous 1874 hoax. Two years later, Jerry Thomas notes that the Tom Collins no longer calls exclusively for gin, and he gives recipes for a Tom Collins Whiskey, Tom Collins Brandy, and so on. The Colonel Collins is the bourbon incarnation, but a bartender may give you a funny look if you order one. In current barspeak, you'll want to order a John Collins, the whiskey version, and then specify bourbon.

COLLINS

2 ounces Fighting Cock bourbon
¾ ounce simple syrup (page 17)
¾ ounce lemon juice
club soda
orange wheel and cocktail cherry for garnish

Shake first three ingredients with ice and strain into a Collins glass filled with ice. Top with club soda, garnish with an orange wheel and cocktail cherry, and serve with a straw.

FUN FACT

In the Tom Collins Hoax of 1874, a speaker asked of a listener, "Have you seen Tom Collins?" When the listener said that he didn't know the man, the speaker reported that Collins was talking about the listener, saying troubling things, just around the corner— usually in a local bar. The listener ran off to find the man, who of course never existed.

RICKEY

The Rickey originated as a highball—bourbon, lime juice, club soda—at Shoomaker's bar in Washington, D.C., in the 1880s. It takes its name from the lobbyist Colonel Joseph Rickey, a Civil War veteran who popularized it. It was an unusual drink at the time and remains so today because lime juice and dark spirits don't often go together. The Rickey took off a decade after its creation, when in the 1890s bartenders dropped the whiskey in favor of gin. The Gin Rickey became a nationwide hit, and even soda shops offered a nonalcoholic version. The bourbon original remained a mostly obscure footnote to cocktail history until political commentator Rachel Maddow made one on *The Martha Stewart Show* on Election Night 2008. That same year, the D.C. Craft Bartenders Guild formed and soon designated July as Rickey Month. Since then, they have celebrated the district's native cocktail by holding annual Rickey competitions for local bartenders.

HIGHBALL

2 ounces Elijah Craig bourbon
¾ ounce lime juice
club soda
lime for garnish

Build the bourbon and lime juice in highball glass filled with ice. Top with club soda and garnish with a lime wheel.

TIP

If the lime doesn't have any sweetness to it,
add ¼ ounce simple syrup to help the drink along.

WARD 8

This cocktail began life in 1898 to commemorate the election of Martin "The Mahatma" Lomasney to the Massachusetts House of Representatives. Boston's Ward Eight—an area roughly triangulated among the South End, South Boston, and Roxbury—reportedly gave him the votes he needed to win the seat. In the 1930s, the columnist G. Selmer Fougner issued a call for the proper recipe for "Along the Wine Trail," his column in the *New York Sun*. Some 400 readers responded, bearing witness to the drink's widespread popularity at that time. The Ward 8 showcases the versatility of classic cocktails and the adaptability of bourbon in mixed drinks.

COUPE

2 ounces bourbon
½ ounce grenadine (page 16)
½ ounce lemon juice
½ ounce orange juice
cocktail cherry for garnish

Shake with ice and strain into a chilled coupe. Garnish with a cherry—on a Boston flag pick if you can.

TIP

Grenadine is a delicious syrup made from pomegranates. Don't buy the weird red artificial stuff at the store. Make your own; it's worth it.

HOT TODDY

The word "toddy" is a phonetic transcription of the Hindi *tadi*, meaning the sap of the Palmyra palm tree, which is fermented into wine. By 1786, the English word denoted a cocktail consisting of a spirit, hot water, sugar, and spices. Many liqueurs and other spirits began life as medicinal mixtures, but this one has retained that special responsibility—as you probably know if you've endured a winter cold or flu. Some recipes call for tea instead of hot water, and in the Midwest some versions call for hot ginger ale to add the health benefits of ginger to the mix. Just what the doctor ordered.

IRISH
COFFEE MUG

2 ounces bourbon

¾ ounce lemon juice

¾ ounce honey

3 ounces boiling water

lemon and cloves for garnish

Build the room-temperature ingredients in a chafed Irish coffee mug, top with the boiling water, and garnish with a clove-studded lemon wheel.

ALLA'S TODDY

An apple a day keeps the doctor away, and apple brandy counts. Every ingredient in this toddy recipe has a health benefit, and the fresh ginger gives it a beautiful, head-clearing kick. If you have an electric juicer, peel the ginger and run it through. Otherwise, you can find fresh ginger shoots at your local health food store.

IRISH
COFFEE MUG

1 ounce Evan Williams bourbon
1 ounce Laird's Apple Brandy
¾ ounce honey syrup
½ ounce ginger juice
½ ounce lemon juice
½ ounce maple syrup
4 ounces boiling water
lemon and cloves for garnish

Build all the ingredients except the boiling water in a chafed Irish coffee mug. Add the boiling water and garnish with a clove-studded lemon wheel.

LUCKY BOURBON HOT CHOCOLATE

This hot chocolate is lucky because of the marshmallows that go on top of it as a garnish. If you didn't know, here's a game changer: you can buy *just the marshmallows* from Lucky Charms cereal! Your pantry is incomplete without a large bag of them. The Tempus Fugit Crème de Cacao also matters. It makes use of a nineteenth-century recipe that calls for Venezuelan cacao and Mexican vanilla. Of all the crèmes de cacao you can buy, it's by far the best.

IRISH COFFEE MUG

1 ounce bourbon

1 ounce Tempus Fugit Crème de Cacao

2 ounces chocolate syrup (page 16)

5 ounces milk or water

whipped cream and Lucky Charms marshmallows for garnish

Combine all the liquid ingredients in a small pan over medium heat until the mixture almost boils. Transfer to a chafed Irish coffee mug and top with whipped cream and Lucky Charms marshmallows.

MINNESOTA BREAKFAST

This drink rolls every delicious breakfast taste into one mug: bacon, butter, maple, rum, and whiskey. The last two may be more of a bartender's breakfast, but they're still delicious on a cold winter morning. A warming classic loved by many, this hot buttered cocktail hails from a time when certain drinks could double as a meal. It's normally made with rum, but we've opted for bourbon washed with bacon fat—fortifying and satisfying on any day when you need a little bracing.

IRISH
COFFEE MUG

1 ounce bacon bourbon

1 ounce spiced rum

½ ounce Bénédictine

½ ounce maple syrup

3 ounces hot water

1 pat butter

cinnamon stick for garnish

Combine the first six ingredients in a small pan over medium heat until the mixture almost boils. Transfer to a chafed Irish coffee mug and garnish with a cinnamon stick.

BACON BOURBON

Warm 1½ ounces bacon fat in a large plastic or glass container. Pour in bourbon from a 750-ml bottle and stir. Let it sit at room temperature 2 to 3 hours and then place in the freezer for 1 hour. Skim off the fat and rebottle.

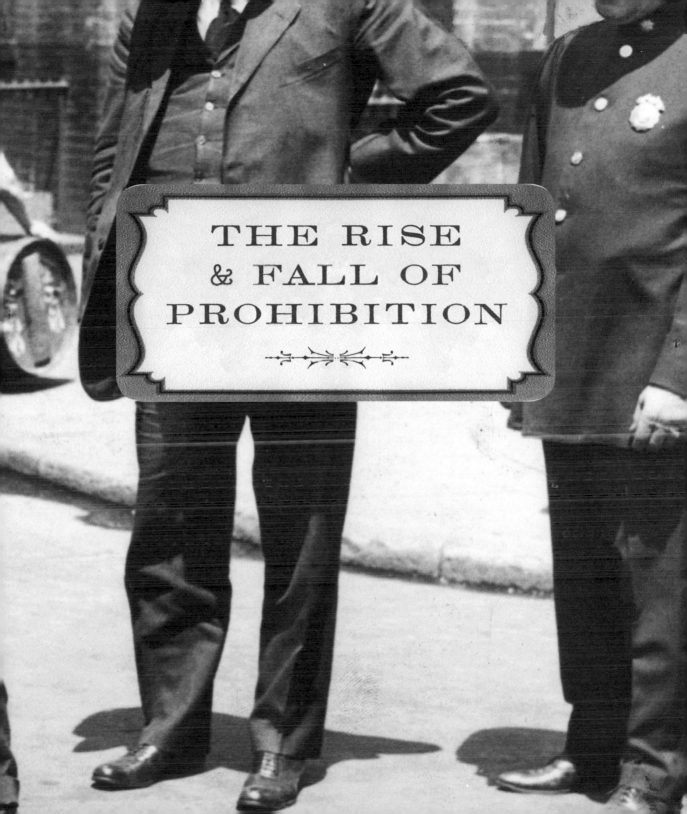

THE RISE
& FALL OF
PROHIBITION

"Prohibition is better than no liquor at all."

–Will Rogers

During the golden age of cocktails, barkeeps rewarded almost any achievement, event, or mood with its own cocktail. When the American explorer Robert Peary reportedly reached the North Pole in 1909, the Arctic Cocktail commemorated his accomplishment with a mixture of sloe gin, red calisaya bark, and orange bitters. The White Plush (whiskey, milk, and seltzer) hoodwinked teetotalers who had requested only milk and seltzer. Many of the creations—passing fads in a boozy flood—didn't survive, but the creative spirit of the age did.

Sporadic temperance movements had plagued early America, but a critical mass began forming in the 1820s and 1830s. The Great War (1914–1918) led to strict controls on the sale of alcohol to aid the war effort, further galvanizing the movement on a national and international level. The U.S. Senate proposed the Eighteenth Amendment in December 1917, and in January 1919 Nebraska supplied the final ratification necessary to amend the Constitution. America officially went dry, but few people stopped drinking. The drys had their law, and the wets had their liquor, as the saying went.

The Volstead Act, which enforced the amendment, featured plenty of loopholes. Pharmacists could dispense whiskey for medicinal purposes to treat almost any ailment. Legislation exempted ecclesiastical wine, so many people found religion. Some people even blended household ingredients into a semblance of hard

PREVIOUS PAGES New York City police supervise the destruction of contraband liquor during the height of Prohibition.

liquor. In 1933, Green & Brothers published *The Secrets of the Liquor Merchant Revealed* by M. I. Fogelsonger, which contains a recipe for Bourbon Whiskey Oil, for adding to grain alcohol, that consists of fusel oil, sulfuric acid, acetate of potassium, dissolved sulfate of copper, oxalate of ammonium, water, and black oxide of magnesium. The ingredients list for the Bourbon Essence recipe doesn't look much better: pelarganic ether, acetate of amyl, rectified fusel oil, extract of orris root, acetic ether, oil of wintergreen, and cologne spirits. Those unsavory blends of poisons clearly weren't keeping people from drinking, but they and other rotgut imitations did change the way Americans drank. To mask the harsh impurities of slapdash hooch, sweetened cocktails were gaining in popularity.

Organized crime also grew at an alarming rate, muscling in on the money that formerly filled government coffers. Gustav Böss, the mayor of Berlin, visited New York City for a week in 1929 and famously asked Mayor James Walker when Prohibition was to go into effect.

The Noble Experiment, as it was called, lasted 13 long years. It helped push cocktail culture to the Caribbean, where it eventually sparked tiki cocktail culture, and to Cuba in particular, where it shone in the sun for a generation before the Cuban Revolution isolated the island nation from America. Prohibition also pushed cocktail culture to Europe, where many disillusioned expats lived between the two world wars. Most Americans fled the threatening storm clouds of fascism in the 1930s, and cocktail culture largely departed with them, but those 13 years in the bars and cafés of London, Paris, and Rome had made their mark.

Stateside, increasingly louder cries for personal freedom and against rising crime and lost revenues finally undermined Prohibition. In December 1933, Utah ratified the Twenty-First Amendment, repealing the Eighteenth, and America raised its collective glass in celebration.

BOULEVARDIER

Harry MacElhone created this drink at Harry's New York Bar on Rue Daunou near the Place Vendôme in Paris in 1927, but much of the credit should go directly to Prohibition itself. When the Volstead Act came into force, MacElhone, a Scot by birth, had to leave New York City and seek work as a barkeep in Europe, where he encountered both Erskine Gwynne and Campari. Gwynne, a writer, socialite, and Vanderbilt relation, published a monthly magazine called *The Boulevardier*. The signature drink that MacElhone created for him riffs on the classic formula of the Manhattan, cleverly using Campari, a bitter Italian liqueur, in lieu of bitters.

COUPE

1½ ounces Russell's Reserve bourbon
¾ ounce Campari
¾ ounce Carpano Antica Formula sweet vermouth
orange for garnish

Stir all the ingredients in a mixing glass filled with ice, strain into a chilled coupe, and garnish with an orange twist.

FUN FACT

MacElhone's family still runs Harry's Bar, so pay it a visit and pay your respects the next time you visit the City of Light.

MILLIONAIRE

This cocktail has a lot of variations without a lot of explanations, much like a lot of cocktail history. One version includes sloe gin, apricot liqueur, and rum. Another combines gin, absinthe, and anisette. This version, created in 1925 at the Carlton Hotel in London, hits the spot and tastes like a million bucks.

COUPE

2 ounces bourbon

½ ounce Grand Marnier

1 ounce grenadine (page 16)

1 egg white

Dry shake all ingredients and then add ice and shake again. Strain into a chilled coupe.

FUN FACT

The Carlton Hotel opened for business in 1899 under the helm of famed Swiss hotelier César Ritz, whose empire inspired the phrase "putting on the ritz." Many millionaires and members of Europe's royal families considered his establishments the only satisfactory places to stay when traveling.

RATTLESNAKE

This drink hails from the legendary *Savoy Cocktail Book* by Harry Craddock, who loved adding absinthe to established drinks. The infamous green liqueur appears in more than 100 cocktails in the book. Here it gives a little extra bite to the Whiskey Sour (page 41), which is made silver by way of an egg white. A friendly bartender once posed this challenge: find a cocktail in which a dash of absinthe would make it worse rather than better. Many years have passed, and we still haven't found one. Behold the magic of modification.

COUPE

1½ ounces bourbon

1 barspoon absinthe

½ ounce simple syrup (page 17)

½ ounce lemon juice

1 egg white

Dry shake all the ingredients, add ice, and shake again. Strain into a chilled coupe.

> **It will either cure Rattlesnake bite, or kill Rattlesnakes, or make you see them.**
>
> –Harry Craddock

SCOFFLAW

"**L**awless drinking is a menace to the republic itself," President Warren Harding famously said, and Delcevare King, a banker and staunch prohibitionist, agreed with him. In 1923, King held a contest to generate a new word describing the lawless drinker of the president's admonition. King appointed members from the Massachusetts Federation of Churches and the Anti-Saloon League of America as cojudges and offered a prize of $200—in addition to bragging rights of course. The contest received more than 25,000 entries, and both Henry Dale and Kate Butler submitted the winner, "scofflaw." They split the money, and a few weeks later this drink appeared at Harry's New York Bar in Paris, where of course Prohibition didn't apply.

COUPE

1½ ounces Noah's Mill bourbon

½ ounce dry vermouth

½ ounce grenadine (page 16)

½ ounce lemon juice

Shake all the ingredients with ice and double strain into a chilled coupe.

FUN FACT

President Harding routinely nipped from
a bottle of whiskey while playing golf.

SEELBACH

Louis and Otto Seelbach opened their eponymous hotel in Louisville, Kentucky, in 1905, and it quickly gained a reputation for its fine grandeur. F. Scott Fitzgerald stayed there, and the hotel served as an inspiration for part of *The Great Gatsby*. In 1995, Adam Seger, head of the hotel's bar and restaurant, discovered this old cocktail recipe and put it back on the menu. Apparently a New Orleans couple were honeymooning at the hotel in 1912, and the groom ordered a Manhattan while the bride opted for a Champagne Cocktail. The bartender spilled some of the latter into the former, and the fortuitous concoction soon became the hotel's signature drink. The rediscovered recipe appeared in *New Classic Cocktails* (1997) by Gaz Regan and spread through the spirits world from there. Seger left the Seelbach in 2001 and then admitted to the *New York Times* in 2016 that he had made the whole thing up for publicity. "How could you have a place that F. Scott Fitzgerald hung out in that doesn't have a damn cocktail?" he said.

COUPE

1 ounce Old Forester 101 bourbon

½ ounce Cointreau

7 dashes Angostura bitters

7 dashes Peychaud's bitters

4 ounces dry sparkling wine

lemon for garnish

Combine all the ingredients except the sparkling wine in a mixing glass filled with ice. Stir 15 to 20 seconds and fine strain into a chilled coupe. Top with sparkling wine and garnish with a lemon twist.

WHISKEY DAISY

daisy is a sour taken to the next level. The Brandy Daisy appeared in the second edition of Jerry Thomas's recipe book, but during the craze and haze of the Jazz Age, bartenders frequently modified the classics. Simple cocktails—spirit, sugar, water, bitters—offered a great place to start, but people wanted more. At the same time, Prohibition limited the resources that bartenders could use, so they had to get creative. Enter this jazzed-up version of a Whiskey Sour, which we like to imagine Daisy Buchanan enjoyed drinking.

WINE

2 ounces Angel's Envy bourbon
½ ounce Curaçao
½ ounce simple syrup (page 17)
1 ounce lemon juice
club soda

Hard shake all the ingredients except the club soda with ice. Strain into a small wineglass filled with ice and top with club soda.

> I wish to live to 150 years old, but the day I die, I wish it to be with a cigarette in one hand and a glass of whiskey in the other.
>
> –Ava Gardner

WHISKEY GIANTS & MAD MEN

"Once during Prohibition I was forced to live for days on nothing but food and water."

-W. C. Fields

When legality limited people's options, they had little reason to care what they were drinking so long as it got them from point A to drunk. After the Twenty-First Amendment repealed Prohibition, they quickly recoiled from the dubious spirits they had been consuming. General categories—bourbon, gin, rye—had sufficed for speakeasy hooch, but after repeal people wanted more than just the basics. Now they began to look for quality. Distilleries that focused on branding, marketing, and reeducation capitalized on those emerging discerning tastes and over the next several decades slowly conglomerated into what became the whiskey giants.

During Prohibition, the federal government had licensed six distilleries to make and sell "medicinal" whiskey. After repeal, those six firms had the perfect foothold from which to launch themselves into the race to sell alcohol commercially again and reestablish brand loyalties. In 1933, these six distilling companies were still standing.

The Wathens, a long-time Kentucky distilling family, consolidated their ongoing whiskey interests into the **American Medicinal Spirits Company** in 1920 and by 1933 owned half of the nation's whiskey distilleries, including Wathen's Distillery and Overholt. AMS sold to National Distillers, which Jim Beam bought in 1987.

George Garvin Brown, a pharmaceutical

PREVIOUS PAGES Businessmen at Gobbler Bar on Madison Avenue in New York City.

salesman, founded **Brown-Forman** in 1870. Today the company owns Old Forester, Woodford Reserve, and numerous other brands.

The Paul Jones Company trademarked the Four Roses brand in 1888 and bought the **Frankfort Distilling Company** in 1922. Seagram acquired it in 1943.

Glenmore—founded in 1849 as the R. Monarch Distillery and acquired in 1901 by the brothers James and Francis Thompson—came under the control of Guinness/United Distillers in 1991.

Lewis Rosenstiel founded the **Schenley Products Company** in the 1920s and subsequently added several distilleries to his portfolio. By 1934, Schenley owned George Dickel, James Pepper, Old Charter, George T. Stagg, and other brands. Rosenstiel's successor sold it to Guinness in 1987.

Weller & Sons, founded 1849, merged with Stitzel Distilling Company, founded 1872, to form **Stitzel-Weller** in 1910. Guinness/United Distillers bought it in the 1980s.

Other notable distilleries opened for business soon after Prohibition ended:

A. Smith Bowman founded his distillery the day after Prohibition ended. Today part of Buffalo Trace/Sazerac, it produces the Virginia Gentleman brand.

The **George T. Stagg Distillery** operated independently of the brand of the same name owned by Schenley (see above). It is now known as the Buffalo Trace Distillery and the Sazerac Company owns it today.

A group of investors formed **Heaven Hill** in 1935. Their brands today include Elijah Craig, Evan Williams, Heaven Hill, and others.

Jim Beam formed in 1933. Today Beam Suntory owns numerous bourbon brands, including Baker's, Basil Hayden, Booker's, Jim Beam, Knob Creek, Maker's Mark, Old Crow, and Old Grand Dad.

Leslie Samuels reopened the family distillery after Prohibition, which led to the creation of **Maker's Mark** some 20 years later.

The future looked bright in 1933, but in 1939 another seminal moment of twentieth-century history stopped the production of bourbon industrywide: the Imperial Japanese Navy bombed Pearl Harbor. Once America joined World War II, all whiskey production ground to a halt in order to help the war effort. Turns out bombs were more important than bourbon. When the war finally ended, a boom time led numerous industries into a golden age of productivity and profits.

From the 1950s to the 1960s, American alcohol consumption increased from 190 million to 235 million gallons annually. By 1967, some 8 million barrels of whiskey were aging across the country. During that time, the cocktail became a symbol of glamour and sophistication. People flocked to new versions of old standards—the Old-Fashioned, Manhattan, Martini, and so on—but a new generation of cocktails emerged from that frenzied growth between the Great Depression and the rise of the counterculture.

OPPOSITE Women on the bottling line at the Stagg Distillery bottling house in Frankfort, Kentucky, in 1941.

ALABAMA SLAMMER

The recipe for this cocktail first appeared in the 1971 *Playboy Bartender's Guide* by Thomas Mario and played a key role in the saga of Southern Comfort, which has a long and fascinating history (page 76). A decade later, bartenders modified the cocktail recipe to conform with changing tastes in alcohol consumption, and soon it became the classic college bar shot of the 1980s. Modern specs often call for orange juice in place of the more traditional lemon juice probably because of the insane popularity of the Tequila Sunrise (made famous in the 1970s by Bill Graham and the Rolling Stones). Pretty much every bar had a bottle or carton of OJ on hand but probably not lemon juice. This recipe rescues the slammer from its shoddy shot phase and returns it to its highball origins. Play "Alabama Song" by the Doors and sip it on a hot and steamy southern summer night.

HIGHBALL

1 ounce amaretto
1 ounce Southern Comfort
½ ounce sloe gin
½ ounce lemon juice

Shake all the ingredients with ice and strain into a highball glass filled with big ice.

VARIATION

For a more visually appealing version, layer the gin at the bottom of the drink. Add it to the empty glass, shake the rest of the ingredients with ice, and then slowly strain them down the back of a barspoon. Make sure to shake up the gin layer as you drink it to have some fun with it and make it taste right.

SOUTHERN COMFORT

This college shot—practically a rite of passage for young adults today—has a long and venerable history as a bottled cocktail. Martin Wilkes Heron created it in 1874 in McCauley's Tavern near Bourbon Street in the French Quarter of New Orleans. The original recipe looked something like this:

  1 bottle bourbon
  ⅛ vanilla bean
  ¼ lemon
  ½ cinnamon stick
  4 cloves
  2 to 3 cherries
  1 or 2 pieces of orange

and its original name was Cuffs and Buttons, probably because of the shapes of the ingredients that went into it. That mixture infused for several days, and then at the very end of the process Heron added honey to sweeten the deal. This cocktail in a bottle packed quite a wallop, so McCauley's Tavern featured a sign that read: TWO PER CUSTOMER. NO GENTLEMAN WOULD ASK FOR MORE. In 1889, Heron moved to Memphis, Tennessee, and patented his concoction. The bottles featured the tagline "None Genuine But Mine."

After Prohibition ended, this solo sipper became its own kind of base spirit. In 1939, David Selznick released *Gone with the Wind*, Victor Fleming's film adaptation of the 1936 bestselling novel by Margaret Mitchell. An honorary cocktail followed. The Scarlett O'Hara contains Southern Comfort, cranberry juice, and lime juice, and it reintroduced a generation of drinkers to Heron's infusion. More cocktails ensued. The Bel-Air contains Southern Comfort, dry vermouth, and lime juice, and the R.A.F. Salute to a Spitfire features Southern Comfort, Jamaican rum, lemon juice, and orange juice.

In the 1980s, shots hit the big time, and SoCo, as the brand became lovingly known, shacked up with lime, either as a squeeze of juice in the shot glass or as a wedge chaser. A generation of college kids overdid it—as only unsupervised young adults can do—relegating Southern Comfort to dorm room or frat house parties or stories of excesses past. But that hasn't stopped new waves of college kids from discovering the same love-hate relationship with SoCo and lime since then.

In 2016, the Brown-Forman Corporation sold the Southern Comfort brand to the Sazerac Company, returning it to its Crescent City origins.

FUN FACT

Janis Joplin's drink of choice was Southern Comfort, and the brand gave her a lynx coat in gratitude. In a less grateful mood, she once smashed a bottle of it over Jim Morrison's head.

BOILERMAKER

While we're on the topic of shots, let's discuss the Boilermaker. A shot of whiskey and a cold beer—it's a simple, undeniably gratifying pairing. The men who built, maintained, and worked with the boilers of the steam-driven locomotives in the 1800s reportedly drank this tasty combination after a long day of work. The Boilermaker has gained in popularity in the years since then. It found new traditional life as a bartender's shift drink at the end of the night while he or she was breaking down the bar and closing out checks. From that vantage point, it has taken on a whole new spin. More recently bartenders and beverage directors have been pairing the two ingredients together carefully—the ideal whiskey with the perfect beer—so the subtle nuances of each enhance the other, giving a highbrow treatment to a lowbrow tradition. Some bar menus now feature entire sections devoted to this pairing. Go on, give it a shot.

SHOT   BEER

1½ ounces Maker's Mark bourbon
1 pint pilsner, such as Victory Prima Pils

Shoot the whiskey, then sip the beer.

FUN FACT

When you drop the shot glass directly into the beer,
it's called a bomb or depth charge.

THE SAMUELS FAMILY MAKES ITS MARK

Robert Samuels arrived in Kentucky in the days of the Whiskey Rebellion in the early 1790s, just as the Bluegrass State joined the Union. Grandson T. W. Samuels built a distillery a stone's throw from the one owned and operated by the Böhm family, who later changed their name to Beam.

After the end of Prohibition, Leslie Samuels reopened the family business and began distilling the family recipe once again. His son, Bill Samuels Sr., wanted to take the company in a new direction by creating a new recipe and using different production techniques that focused on product quality rather than batch frequency. But Leslie, eager to resume operations after the long dry spell, brushed aside his son's suggestions and resumed distilling as before. The product wasn't top shelf, but consumers were eager to drink and ready to buy.

Then Bill Sr. finally had his chance. He sold the family's existing setup and used the profits to buy the historic Burks Spring Distillery in 1953. In a dramatic farewell to past tradition, Bill Sr. burned the old family recipe and, with the help of the greater bourbon community—including master distillers such as Jerry Beam, Hap Motlow, Ed Shapiro, and Pappy van Winkle—worked on creating a new recipe. His goal seems obvious: produce quality whiskey

that tastes good. One major change was using red winter wheat in the mash bill. The next year production of Maker's Mark began.

Bill's wife, Maggie, was responsible for the name and the distinctive packaging. She collected English pewter, which required discovering, examining, and understanding the maker's marks—a form of sculptural trademark recognition—on the pieces. She then designed a distinctive maker's mark for her husband's bourbon. They used a unique bottle, dipping the neck in red wax like a Cognac, and priced their whiskey to reflect the premium product that the bottle contained. In 1958, the first bottles of

Maker's Mark released for sale. The new bourbon became a hit locally, but the high price and low name recognition led to poor sales overall. The Samuelses had to take risks and make waves.

One of those risks was an ad with the tagline "It tastes expensive . . . and is." They also struck a deal with major airlines to secure a place as the exclusive bourbon available in the beverage carts. When Bill Sr. passed the business to his son, Bill Jr., in 1975, he offered one admonition: "Don't screw up the whiskey."

Bill Jr. did as he was told and took the marketing to a new level, including dressing up as a clown and juggling bottles. Marketing gimmicks aside, the family dedication to quality continued and reaped huge rewards. The brand passed through a series of corporate hands: Hiram Walker, Fortune Brands, Beam, Inc., and now Suntory. Maker's Mark weathered bourbon's dark age (page 106) and survived to flourish in the bourbon renaissance that the visionary Bill Sr. had anticipated years earlier.

BROWN DERBY

This iconic Los Angeles restaurant chain opened in 1926 and in its day was the place to be seen. When Lucy, Fred, and Ethel visit the Brown Derby in the "Hollywood at Last" episode of *I Love Lucy* (February 1955), a starstruck Lucy manages to get William Holden hit with a pie. But the story goes that the cocktail really originated at the Vendome Club in Hollywood, helmed by entrepreneur and restaurateur Billy Wilkerson, who also founded the *Hollywood Reporter*, the Flamingo Hotel, and Ciro's nightclub in addition to discovering Lana Turner. Cocktail historians have recognized the similarities between the Brown Derby and De Rigueur cocktails for a while. The De Rigueur appeared in Judge Jr.'s *Here's How* (1927) and called for scotch. Harry Craddock's *Savoy Cocktail Book* (1930) picked it up and simplified the spirit to whiskey. A few years later, another book, *Hollywood Cocktails*—published by a greeting card company that heavily repeated Craddock—also included the recipe. In Craddock, the Derby precedes the De Rigueur, so perhaps the folks at the card company accidentally skipped repeating an entry. Either way, recipes for this cocktail frequently omit the lemon juice and go easy on the honey. Because the sugar content in varieties of grapefruit differs drastically, we've included a small amount of lemon juice that you can adjust, depending on the grapefruit you use. The same idea applies to the honey. If you substitute straight honey, use less. A rich honey syrup requires a little more, and our honey syrup a little more than that.

COUPE

2 ounces Jefferson's bourbon

¾ ounce honey syrup (page 17)

1 ounce grapefruit juice

¼ ounce lemon juice

Shake all the ingredients with ice and double strain into a chilled coupe.

COCK & BULL

Anglophile American John Morgan founded this legendary restaurant on the Sunset Strip in Los Angeles in 1937, and over the decades, among the roster of Hollywood celebrity regulars, it also attracted a Who's Who of British expats, including Somerset Maugham, Richard Burton, and Rod Stewart. This venerable venue also hosted the creation of a renowned twentieth-century cocktail, the Moscow Mule (more about that on page 95). The Cock & Bull cocktail never reached the same lofty cultural heights as the Mule, but it can more than hold its own as a delicious drink. The original Cock & Bull restaurant shut its doors in 1987. Another British pub by the same name opened in Santa Monica three years later, but you won't find this drink on its menu, so here's how to make your own.

ROCKS

¾ ounce Bénédictine

¾ ounce Michter's bourbon

½ ounce Cognac

¼ ounce dry Curaçao

1 dash Angostura bitters

orange for garnish

Stir all the ingredients in a mixing glass filled with ice for 15 seconds and strain into a rocks glass filled with big ice. Garnish with an orange twist.

THE DERBY

Horse races and hats, that's all cocktail names really are, and this recipe comes to us from Trader Vic. Victor Bergeron Jr. suffered from ill health as a young man but eventually found work in his uncle's bar. The two men had a falling out, however, and Vic borrowed money from his aunt to open his own bar, Hinky Dink's, nearby, which he decorated to look like—*wait for it*—an Alaskan hunting lodge. A visit to the Don the Beachcomber restaurant in Los Angeles during the Great Depression turned him on to the draw of a more relaxed vibe and more colorful cocktails. He suggested that he and Ernest Gantt (aka Don the Beachcomber) form a partnership, but Gantt declined. In 1938, Bergeron visited Cuba and met the man who later became his mentor, Constantino Ribalaigua i Vert, owner of the celebrated Bar La Florida. Trader Vic, as Bergeron became known, launched a tiki empire that continues to this day. Among his many cocktail creations, the Mai Tai is arguably the most famous and most controversial. Both he and Gannt claimed the bragging rights for inventing it. This recipe appeared in his 1947 *Bartender's Guide*. The Curaçao and lime juice give the bourbon a nice Caribbean twist.

COUPE

1 ounce Noah's Mill bourbon

½ ounce Carpano Antica Formula sweet vermouth

½ ounce Curaçao

½ ounce lime juice

mint sprigs for garnish

Shake all the liquid ingredients with ice and double strain into a chilled coupe. Garnish with mint.

VARIATION

Replace the Curaçao with a split combination—¼ ounce each of Cointreau and Grand Marnier—for a slightly sweeter version of the drink.

THE DYING BASTARD

The Dying Bastard and the Dead Bastard form part of a trilogy created by Joe Scialom at the Shepheard Hotel in Cairo in the early 1940s. During World War II, the Nazis were closing in on the city, cutting off its access to decent spirits. Soldiers—who have a timeless proclivity for drinking and one of the best justifications for it—complained about the terrible hangovers that shoddy booze was giving them. Scialom heard their pleas and gave them a solution to their ills, the Suffering Bastard (see opposite). It conquered their pains so well that at one point the troops requested more from the front lines, sending him a telegram: "Can you please send eight gallons of Suffering Bastard, everyone is really hungover." Scialom dutifully obliged, filling every container he could find and flagging every available taxi to ferry the concoction to them. If you have a hangover that a Suffering Bastard just won't cure, make yourself a Dying Bastard. Here's how.

ROCKS

½ ounce Maker's Mark bourbon

½ ounce brandy

½ ounce gin

¾ ounce ginger syrup (page 16)

¾ ounce lime juice

2 dashes Angostura bitters

orange and mint sprigs for garnish

Shake all the ingredients with ice and strain into a rocks glass filled with ice. Garnish with an orange slice and mint.

66 **Isn't anything Ah got whiskey won't cure.** 99

–William Faulkner

THE SUFFERING BASTARD

The Suffering Bastard doesn't contain any bourbon, but the recipe is worth noting for the family's sake. The original calls for 3 ounces of ginger ale, which we've modified below.

1 ounce brandy
1 ounce gin
½ ounce ginger syrup (page 16)
¼ ounce demerara syrup (page 16)
¾ ounce lime juice
  club soda
1 dash Angostura bitters
  orange and mint sprigs for garnish

Dry shake all the ingredients except the club soda and bitters and strain into a rocks glass. Top with club soda and fill with crushed ice. Add a dash of bitters to the ice. Garnish with mint and an orange wheel and serve with a straw.

THE DEAD BASTARD

When all else fails—well, here you go.

½ ounce Maker's Mark bourbon
½ ounce brandy
½ ounce gin
½ ounce rum
¾ ounce ginger syrup (page 16)
¾ ounce lime juice
1 dash Angostura bitters
  orange and mint sprigs for garnish

Shake all the ingredients with ice and strain into a rocks glass filled with ice. Garnish with an orange slice and mint.

THE BURIED BASTARD

We don't give up easily, so if you succeed in working your way through Scialom's deadly threesome, you're probably going to need our addition to the family.

½ ounce Appleton Estate Signature rum
½ ounce Booker's bourbon
½ ounce Plymouth gin
½ ounce ginger syrup (page 16)
½ ounce lime juice
½ ounce Angostura bitters
  orange and mint sprigs for garnish

Shake all the ingredients with ice and strain into a rocks glass filled with ice. Garnish with orange slice and mint.

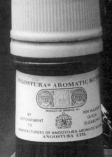

FANCY FREE

eatured in Crosby Gaige's 1941 *Cocktail Guide and Ladies' Companion*, this drink hearkens back to the Old-Fashioned but with maraschino liqueur substituting for the sugar, the same way that Ernest Hemingway preferred his Daiquirís (maraschino as a sweetener in place of sugar). At one point, the recipe called for a sugared rim, but if you're old enough to drink, you're old enough to drink this like Papa Hemingway—without sugar.

ROCKS

2 ounces Four Roses Single Barrel bourbon

½ ounce Luxardo maraschino liqueur

2 dashes Angostura bitters

2 dashes orange bitters

lemon for garnish

Stir all the ingredients in a mixing glass filled with ice and strain into a rocks glass filled with big ice. Garnish with a lemon twist.

FUN FACT

Crosby Gaige was an author, theater producer, and president of the New York Wine and Food Society.

FRISCO

Joe Frisco was a famous vaudeville performer, jazz dancer, and stuttering comic. F. Scott Fitzgerald mentions him when describing the guests at one of Gatsby's infamous parties: "Suddenly one of these gypsies in trembling opal seizes a cocktail out of the air, dumps it down for courage and moving her hands like Frisco dances out alone on the canvas platform." In 2010, Frank Bruni wrote about his quest for the Frisco recipe in the pages of the *New York Times*, consulting cocktail guru Jim Meehan, who "said that a Frisco recipe from the early part of the twentieth century mentioned whiskey, without specifying what type, and Bénédictine. Frisco recipes from the 1940s, he said, specifically call for bourbon." Fitzgerald died in 1940 and Frisco in 1958, but we imagine both of them tipping one or two of these back as liquid courage for a rollicking night in their jittery world of racetracks, hotels, restaurants, theaters, and clubs.

COUPE

2 ounces Buffalo Trace bourbon
½ ounce Bénédictine

Shake with ice and strain into a chilled coupe.

VARIATION

For a **FRISCO SOUR**, you'll need a high-rye bourbon.
Four Roses Single Barrel has the mash bill with the highest rye content
(35 percent), but you can use Basil Hayden, Bulleit, or Old Grand Dad.

2 ounces Four Roses Single Barrel bourbon
½ ounce Bénédictine
½ ounce lemon juice

Make as above.

KENTUCKY MULE

John Martin of the Hartford-based Heublein Brothers distribution company and Jack Morgan, owner of the Cock & Bull restaurant on Sunset Boulevard in Los Angeles, kicked the Moscow Mule into existence in 1941 by combining vodka, ginger beer, and a squeeze of lime. Substitute bourbon for the vodka and you have a Kentucky Mule. The rich, smooth sweetness of the bourbon's caramel and vanilla notes tempers the bright zing of the ginger and lime. The result? The most delicious ginger snap cookie you've ever drunk.

COPPER MUG

2 ounces bourbon
¾ ounce ginger beer
¾ ounce lime juice
club soda
candied ginger or lime for garnish

Whip shake all the ingredients except the club soda. Pour into a copper mug filled with ice. Top with club soda, garnish with candied ginger or a lime wedge, and serve with a straw.

FUN FACT

Kentucky produces approximately 95 percent of the country's bourbon but ironically boasts a large number of dry counties. Of 120 counties total, 38 are *completely* dry and another 49 are dry with special circumstances.

KENTUCKY BOURBON TRAIL

The members of the Kentucky Distillers Association banded together in 1880 to fight against regulation. Prohibition nearly killed the organization until they turned on the Noble Experiment itself. They lobbied for repeal, and by 1936 the KDA was back in action. In 1999, they introduced the Kentucky Bourbon Trail, the so-called Napa Valley of spirits. It's less a trail and more of a general area that many distilleries, scattered between Louisville and Lexington, call home. Since then the bourbon industry has grown. Established distilleries, big and small, are expanding, while new enterprises are just laying distillate in barrels. No animosity exists between the old guard and the new. As we heard at Maker's Mark, you never know who the next Bill Samuels may be.

Most distilleries offer a facilities tour, an incredible experience in the mecca of bourbon.

ANGEL'S ENVY distills in a fancy new building on Whiskey Row in Lousiville. They joined the trail in 2017, but the bourbon made here won't release for sale until 2020.

BULLEIT also just opened their distillery, and you can visit the Bulleit Frontier Whiskey Experience at the old Stitzel-Weller distillery.

At the **EVAN WILLIAMS** Bourbon Experience on Whiskey Row, you can visit their artisanal distillery, take a guided tour, and of course taste their delicious spirits.

FOUR ROSES was a national favorite until Seagram's bought them in the 1950s and used the brand to hawk below-average Canadian whisky while exporting the good stuff to Japan. Kirin bought them in 2002 and quickly righted the ship. The distillery tour will teach you a lot about mash bills and yeast strains. That, and they make damn good whiskey.

HEAVEN HILL makes around 900 barrels of whiskey per day in Louisville proper—with plans to increase that number to 1,200—and has more than 50 rickhouses in Bardstown to store all of it. They also have a smaller operation on Whiskey Row, where a longtime distiller makes just one barrel a day, the old-fashioned way.

JIM BEAM also has a huge distillery complex as well as a craft operation, where they make experimental batches and have a room featuring many decanters that the company released from the 1950s to the 1990s. Fun fact: the genie bottle in *I Dream of Jeannie* is a Jim Beam decanter.

Driving to **MAKER'S MARK** will give you a feeling for the vision that Margie Samuels had for preserving the history of the distillery that she and her husband purchased in the early 1950s: equal parts idyllic and industrial, tradition and innovation.

The first distillery built in Lexington after a century hiatus, **TOWN BRANCH** features both a brewery and distillery.

WILD TURKEY has approximately 6 million barrels of whiskey at any given time—in a state with just 4.4 million people—and offers tours just about every hour. They've used the same strain of yeast since 1950, and at the tasting they'll teach you the Kentucky Chew, the Jimmy Russel–approved method of tasting whiskey.

You can't escape the beauty of bourbon country, but the postcard-perfect drive to WOODFORD RESERVE will take your breath away. Maybe the stark contrast with New York City's browns and grays made the Kentucky landscape seem more picturesque, more lush, more green. Either way, try their bourbon balls and double-oaked whiskey.

Not all area distilleries belong to the Bourbon Trail. BUFFALO TRACE, for example, decided not to participate. When Colonel Edmund Haynes Taylor purchased the distillery, he called it "O.F.C." because he believed the best whiskey came from old-fashioned copper stills. George T. Stagg bought it a few years later, and Albert Blanton began working here as an office boy in 1897.

The WILLETT family got into distilling just after Prohibition, but the distillery closed in 1980. Even Kulsveen married into the Willett Family and restarted the business, which rejoined the KDA in 2012.

Expanding on its success, the KDA also has a Kentucky Bourbon Trail Craft Tour, which includes Barrel House, Bluegrass, Boone County, Corsair, Hartfield, Kentucky Artisan, Kentucky Peerless, Limestone Branch, M. B. Roland, New Riff, Old Pogue, Wilderness Trail, and Willett. Louisville's Urban Bourbon Trail highlights 35 bars and restaurants that feature bourbon-focused menus, many of which use the spirit in interesting and exciting cocktails.

LION'S TAIL

On his second voyage to the New World, after making landfall on Jamaica, Christopher Columbus encountered allspice berries. The English later gave the plant the name we use because the berry's complex flavor seemed to contain cinnamon, nutmeg, and clove all in one, although it also goes by the name Jamaican pepper. (The English wrested control of Jamaica from the Spanish in 1655 and held it as part of the British Empire until the island gained full independence in 1962.) Allspice proved enormously popular in America from 1930 to 1970, coinciding nicely with the first sighting of this classic recipe in the 1937 *Café Royal Cocktail Book* by William Tarling, president of the United Kingdom Bartenders Guild, and stretching to the end of the second wave of tiki cocktail culture.

COUPE

1½ ounces Jim Beam Black Double Barrel bourbon

½ ounce lime

¼ ounce allspice dram

½ ounce simple syrup (page 17)

2 dashes Angostura bitters

Shake all the ingredients with ice and double strain into a chilled coupe.

MONTE CARLO

In *The Fine Art of Mixing Drinks*, David Embury lists the six standard drinks that everyone should know how to make: Old-Fashioned, Manhattan, Martini, Jack Rose, Sidecar, and Daiquirí. Once you understand how and why these six drinks work, substituting base liquors, sweeteners, citrus, and other foundational components opens up a world of new cocktails. In his own way, he's teaching people the art of the bartender's choice. Embury totally rejects the idea that a drink must be made according to one exact recipe. The final arbiter always should be your taste. To that end, he suggests trying different ratios, finding the one that most pleases you, and sticking with it. In that same spirit, we present this scion of the Bénédictine-bourbon family as a Manhattan variant, with the sweet liqueur subbing for sweet vermouth. Take a gamble. We bet you'll like it.

ROCKS

2 ounces Buffalo Trace bourbon
½ ounce Bénédictine
2 dashes Angostura Bitters
lemon for garnish

Stir all the liquid ingredients in a mixing glass filled with ice for 15 seconds, strain into a rocks glass filled with big ice, and garnish with a lemon twist.

PICKLEBACK

There's something about shots that requires the even symmetry of a one-two punch. If you're having a shot, you're going to want a chaser. Russia has vodka and pickles. Mexico has tequila and pickles. Now America has bourbon and pickles. This southwestern standard made its way to Brooklyn, where the combo gained real traction along with a name for itself. Reggie Cunningham was working a shift at Bushwick Country Club and encountered an unorthodox request. While having a snack of McClure's pickles, stored in the bar's basement, a bar patron requested a shot of the pickle juice to go along with her whiskey. At first, the idea repulsed Cunningham, and so the customer offered him one. Ten or so shots of whiskey and pickle juice made him a true believer. Not only did Cunningham claim that it cured his cold, he also said that he didn't have a hangover the next day. Sounds like a drink that has earned its place in cocktail history.

SHOT

1½ ounces Old Crow bourbon

1 ounce McClure's Spicy Pickle Spears brine

Pour the two ingredients into separate shot glasses. Shoot the whiskey, then the pickle brine. Repeat as necessary.

THE
ROMAN TWIST

Joe Scialom served as head bartender at the Shepheard Hotel in Cairo until local officials arrested the Italian national because of his Jewish ancestry. In 1952, mass rioting caused the Cairo Fire, in which the hotel burned down. When it reopened after the Suez Crisis in 1956, the *New York Times* noted that Scialom wasn't returning with it. "One of the latter day fixtures of the old Shepheard's that was to be transplanted to the new hotel was a casualty of the Suez war. That fixture was the famed Joe, who officiated with such dexterity and sympathetic understanding at what was called the Long Bar." After fleeing Egypt, Scialom worked on many of Conrad Hilton's projects, including the Cavalieri Hilton in Rome, where Scialom created this drink in 1963.

COUPE

1¼ ounces bourbon

1 ounce Tia Maria

1 ounce orgeat (see page 17)

1 ounce lemon juice

1 ounce orange juice

Shake all the ingredients with ice and strain into a chilled coupe.

STONE FENCE

One of our favorite pairings of a shot and a pint is also one of the oldest. The Stone Fence dates back to the Revolutionary War. At the southern end of Lake Champlain on what is now the border between New York and Vermont, the Green Mountain Boys—led by Ethan Allen of future furniture fame—captured Fort Ticonderoga from the British. Before doing so, they downed several Stone Fences. At that time the drink probably contained rum, but as America separated itself from the triangular trade with British sugar plantations in the Caribbean, over time whiskey became the spirit of choice. Call it a cider bomb if you like, but Stone Fence has a proper solid ring to it, and as Robert Frost, onetime poet laureate of Vermont, once acknowledged: Good fences make good neighbors.

BEER

2 ounces bourbon

5 ounces hard cider

Pour the bourbon into a beer glass and top with the cider.

THE DARK AGES

"Middle-aged, middle-class, whiskey-drinking, bluenosed bureaucrats."

–Timothy Leary, 1966

As the baby boomers aged into adulthood in the 1960s and early 1970s, consumer taste in alcohol, like everything else in America, underwent an enormous paradigm shift. Between 1960 and 1975, whiskey's market share dropped from 74 percent to 54 percent. At the same time, the "clears"—vodka, unaged rum, and tequila—climbed from 19 percent to 35 percent.

Vodka brands, with their antiestablishment hint of forbidden Russian origins, suddenly became the cool kids on the market, diametrically opposing grandpa's stuffy whiskey. Marketing companies did everything in their power to convince consumers that one vodka tasted better than the next . . . or rather tasted less since the Alcohol and Tobacco Tax and Trade Bureau defined it as a colorless, odorless, tasteless spirit. Origin stories and fresh ingredients didn't matter to young consumers looking into the future. Economic decline murdered the three-Martini lunch. Packaging ruled supreme.

In that new atmosphere, bartenders invented the shooter. As a measure of drinking responsibly, the shot has always been with us, but shooters aren't shots. They're mixed drinks made by the ounce or two, slapped with a catchy name, and thrown back for quick inebriation. Blowjob, Buttery Nipple, Kamikaze, Pink Squirrel, Redheaded Slut—these represent just a few of the offensive monstrosities that we pulled from the wreckage of the era. Even whiskey itself couldn't escape the spirit of the age.

In a bid to compete with the clear spirits, American whiskey producers sought permission to make "light whiskey." They wanted to use whatever mash bill they wanted, to distill up to an essence-obliterating 160 proof, and to reuse barrels to make a product that would appeal to changing tastes, particularly among young people and women. Essentially, they wanted to create whiskey-flavored vodka. In February 1973, Lady Like Light Whiskey debuted with the tagline "Love in a bottle." Thankfully, this crass

commercial attempt to debase good whiskey in favor of fickle tastes didn't catch on, but whiskey producers worldwide still faced the problem of lost market share.

Absolut rode an ingenious marketing campaign to record profits in the mid-1980s, prompting more and more brands to enter the market. At the same time, Seagram created a line of schnapps branded with the face of the fictitious Aloysius Percival McGillicuddy. This "world-famous" nineteenth-century physician, also known as the shot doctor, sported Victorian facial hair and promulgated vaguely pharmaceutical beverages, such as Mentholmint and Black Licorice schnapps. Into that mix, Seagram added Dr. McGillicuddy's Fireball Whisky. It was Canadian and so not a bourbon, but even the Canadians lost interest in the prospect. Conceding defeat, Seagram sold the brand to the Sazerac Company in 1989. But that didn't mark the end of bourbon's popularity. It turns out that vodka producers were going to sow the seeds of their own downfall.

CRAFT DISTILLING & COCKTAILS

"The purpose of drinking is to get as drunk as you can without ruining it for other people."

–Sasha Petraske

Bill Samuels Sr. launched Maker's Mark in 1958, paying careful attention to detail and quality some 40 years ahead of the curve, but the first real stirrings of today's bourbon renaissance reach back to 1984. That year Elmer T. Lee became master distiller at the George T. Stagg Distillery (now Buffalo Trace) and created Blanton's, the world's first single-barrel bourbon. Working alongside Lee was Booker Noe, grandson of Jim Beam. Noe had stashes of Booker's Bourbon that employees, friends, and guests enjoyed, but he never sold it because no one thought there was a market for it.

In 1987, the president of Jim Beam was looking for a gift to give to key distributors. Booker's came to mind. They poured it into some old wine bottles, added a personal note from Booker Noe, and sent them out. After tasting it, the distributors wanted to sell this delicious private stock. Neither cut nor filtered, Booker's hit the market the next year. Knob Creek, Basil Hayden, and Woodford Reserve soon followed.

At the same time, renowned restaurateur Joe Baum told Dale DeGroff to find a copy of Jerry Thomas's book (page 32) and use it to create drinks for a new classic cocktail bar in the Rainbow Room restaurant atop 30 Rockefeller Center. DeGroff's focus on quality ingredients mirrored the same emphasis in the bourbon distilleries. A fruitful partnership began and gained momentum.

After the major players began reintroducing quality bourbon to the market, craft distillers and microdistillers joined the game—as did home distillers after the Great Recession shook up America's workforce in 2008.

Not all of these craft brands are created equal, however. A Lawrenceburg, Indiana, distillery founded in 1847 came under Seagram control in 1933. When Seagram sank, Pernod Ricard bought the facility, which eventually passed to Midwest Grain Products. MGP creates spirits for sale to other companies—including Diageo, its largest client—which sell it under roughly 50 different brand names. Whiskey expert Chuck Cowdery calls these bottling companies "Potemkin distilleries," though some of them do process the MGP product before selling it. Sometimes these whiskeys have interesting labels and cute backstories about some fabricated distilling ancestor, but the liquid still comes from MGP.

Nevertheless, it's not hard to find good-quality bourbon from legitimate craft distillers. According to the American Distilling Institute, the country had fewer than 30 craft distillers around the turn of the millennium. Today it has more than 750.

Let's celebrate that incredible renaissance with a few cocktails.

AUNTIE ROSE

Bourbon goes floral. Following the theme, we use Four Roses, a spirit that nicely exemplifies the history of bourbon in America. Four Roses Yellow Label proved enormously popular in the 1930s and 1940s, and the Frankfort Distilling Company sold the brand to Seagram in 1943. A little more than a decade later, Seagram redirected its efforts toward blended whiskey, shifting the brand name stateside to a blended whiskey of questionable character and shifting the bourbon proper to overseas markets, where it reigned as a bestseller, particularly in Japan. Diageo bought most of the Seagram brands in 2002 and then sold Four Roses to the Japanese beverage company Kirin (part of Mitsubishi). Master distiller Jim Rutledge asked Kirin to bring the bourbon back to American shelves, and it returned triumphant in 2004.

COUPE

1½ ounces Four Roses bourbon
½ ounce falernum
¾ ounce rose syrup (page 17)
½ ounce lemon juice
edible roses for garnish

Hard shake all the ingredients with ice, double strain into a coupe, and garnish with fresh or dried edible roses.

TIP

You can find dried edible roses in spice shops and online.
They make a nice floral syrup and a great garnish.

BERMUDA TRIANGLE

In *Beachbum Berry's Grog Log*, Tiki guru Jeff Berry notes the Test Pilot cocktail as a Don the Beachcomber invention that dates to around 1941, when American pilots were sailing to foreign shores to fight the Germans and the Japanese. That recipe called for Jamaican rum, Puerto Rican rum, Cointreau, Pernod, falernum, lime juice, and Angostura bitters and spawned a number of variations, including the Ace Pilot, the Astronaut, and the Space Pilot. Its most famous offshoot remains the Jet Pilot, however, a classic tiki drink that Berry traces to the Beverly Hills Luau restaurant in 1958. This updated variation reinterprets the Beachcomber original and contains a trio of New World spirits: apple brandy from America's first distillery, bourbon of course, and a big ol' Jamaican rum. Frank Cisneros brought this cocktail to our attention, and it tastes like a goddamn miracle. One of us even fell in love with an ex-husband over this drink. Drinker beware.

ROCKS

1 ounce Laird's Apple Brandy

1 ounce Old Bardstown bourbon

¾ ounce Smith & Cross rum

½ ounce falernum

½ ounce cinnamon syrup

¾ ounce orange juice

½ ounce lemon juice

8 dashes St. Elizabeth Allspice Dram

4 dashes absinthe

2 dashes Angostura bitters

mint sprigs and cinnamon stick for garnish

Whip shake all ingredients and strain into a rocks glass filled with crushed ice. Garnish with mint sprigs and freshly grated cinnamon and serve with a straw.

BLACK MANHATTAN

This boozy Manhattan variant hails from the best coast West Coast. At San Francisco's Bourbon & Branch, bartender Todd Smith substituted Averna, a Sicilian amaro, for the traditional sweet vermouth in this cocktail (originally named the Harlem). Amaros are bitter liqueurs with a lower alcohol by volume, so they substitute easily for vermouth, a fortified wine, while adding a delicious tang to historically sweet recipes. Averna's flavors focus on orange, liquorice, and Mediterranean herbs sweetened with a hint of caramel, which makes for a full, warming, herbaceous cocktail.

COUPE

2¼ ounces bourbon

¾ ounces Averna

2 dashes Angostura bitters

cocktail cherry for garnish

Stir all the ingredients in a mixing glass filled with ice for 15 seconds. Strain into a chilled coupe and garnish with a cherry.

FUN FACT

Born in Caltanissetta, Sicily, in 1802, Salvatore Averna sourced the recipe for his bitter elixir from Benedictine monks. His son Francesco popularized it, winning royal recognition for the mixture from King Umberto I and then a royal patent from King Vittorio Emanuele III. The Campari Group bought the family company in 2014 for more than 100 million euros.

COUNTRY GENTLEMAN

Whiskey doesn't often go into savory cocktails, and bourbon even less frequently, but by law bourbon must have a mash bill containing at least 51 percent corn. What grows together goes together, so when you think about it, this seemingly unusual pairing makes sense. The bell pepper mellows and sweetens the savory notes of the black salt. Make way for a brunch cocktail with class.

COUPE

2 × 2 inch green bell pepper
10 peppercorns
1½ ounces bourbon
½ ounce Manzanilla Sherry
1 ounce corn puree (page 16)
¾ ounce lemon juice
black salt for rimming
bell pepper for garnish

In a shaking tin, muddle the green bell pepper and peppercorns. Add the liquid ingredients and shake with ice. Rim a chilled coupe with black salt and strain the cocktail into it. Garnish with a bell pepper flower.

TIP

For the bell pepper flower, carefully carve a decorative flower shape from the bell pepper of your choice.

EXPAT

Lauren Schell served as bar manager of Sasha Petraske's legendary New York City bar Milk & Honey—epicenter of the craft cocktail renaissance—and also as head bartender at Little Branch. She created this drink stateside before moving to Melbourne, Australia, in 2011 to open the Everleigh. The Expat takes its refreshing citrus notes from the Daiquirí and nods to the strong elegance of the Julep, which has long demonstrated that bourbon and mint play well together. That winning combination, plus a touch of bitters to balance the ship, forms a whole new elixir experience that's just as refreshing as either, and this is the perfect summer cocktail to sway any finicky whiskey-in-winter drinkers. Schell returned to Manhattan and now directs the beverage program at Grand Banks, an oyster bar on the *Sherman Zwicker*, a wooden schooner moored in the Tribeca neighborhood of Manhattan.

COUPE

6 mint leaves

2 ounces Elijah Craig 12 Year bourbon

¾ ounce simple syrup (page 17)

1 ounce lime juice

2 dashes Angostura bitters

In a shaking tin, muddle the mint and then add the liquid ingredients. Shake with ice and fine strain into a chilled coupe.

GOLD RUSH

Sasha Petraske opened Milk & Honey on Manhattan's Lower East Side in 1999 and catalyzed a chain reaction that completely transformed New York's hospitality and nightlife scene. The culinary world also took note. T. J. Siegal created this simple, sophisticated, stylish drink at Milk & Honey around 2000 and finally gave the classic mixture—which could have been called a sling, sour, or toddy in decades past—a name. That name also nicely describes the stream of speakeasy-style craft cocktail bars that followed Milk & Honey and flooded New York. Petraske's life ended all too soon in 2015, but Siegal's drink and others pay tribute to his singular contribution to the world of cocktails.

ROCKS

2 ounces Elijah Craig bourbon
¾ ounce honey syrup (page 17)
¾ ounce lemon juice

Shake all the ingredients with ice and strain into a chilled rocks glass filled with big ice.

GREEN MONSTER

While home-brewing beer, friends Darek Bell and Andrew Webber ran into trouble and switched to spirits. Their award-winning Corsair Distillery in Nashville—which prides itself on making "hand-crafted, small-batch, ultra-premium booze for badasses"—makes some seriously adventurous whiskeys, including Quinoa Whiskey, Ryemageddon, and Triple Smoke. For Triple Smoke, which *Whisky Advocate* named Artisan Whiskey of the Year in 2013, Corsair smokes its malted barley with beechwood, cherry, and peat, which gives this American whiskey a hearty and complex flavor. The big, herbal flavors of green Chartreuse help balance the drink and give it its name (which doesn't refer to the signature green left-field wall in Boston's Fenway Park).

ROCKS

¾ ounce bourbon

¾ ounce green Chartreuse

½ ounce Corsair Triple Smoke

½ ounce Giffard triple sec

½ ounce lemon juice

mint for garnish

Shake all the ingredients with ice and strain into a rocks glass filled with crushed ice. Garnish with flamed mint and serve with a straw.

GUNS 'N' ROSÉ

It's not a flavor that appears in many bourbon cocktail recipes, but the fresh tropical fruitiness of apricot pairs naturally with the vanilla notes of the bourbon as well as the strawberry flavors found in sparkling rosé. You might even say it forms a delicious musical bridge. The drink takes its name from the band because at some point we had to pay tribute. When she was young, one of us wrote a fan letter to Slash, who sent back an autographed picture. (She still has it and remains very proud of it.) This refreshing spritz is perfect for drinking during rosé weather, but it's amped up so you can rock out with something a little harder than just wine.

COLLINS

¾ ounce Evan Williams bourbon

½ ounce Giffard apricot brandy

¾ ounce lime juice

½ ounce orange juice

2 ounces sparkling rosé

Shake all the ingredients except the sparkling rosé with ice and strain into a Collins glass filled with ice. Top with the sparkling rosé. Garnish with a lime wheel and prepare yourself for a taste of Paradise City.

MARK OF THE BEAST

This bittersweet frenzy originally contained six dashes of each bitters, hence the name. Once we got a hold of ourselves, moderation prevailed, though we still like a shot of Angostura now and then as a digestif. It'll cure what ails you and has helped us through some devilishly extreme circumstances. Bitters are something of a bartender's cure-all, you see. Feeling particularly hellish? Have a club soda with bitters. We created this cocktail for one of those times when club soda just wasn't enough. Add a bottle of bitters to your emergency preparedness kit. Here is wisdom.

ROCKS

2 ounces Kentucky Vintage bourbon
½ ounce honey syrup (page 17)
3 dashes Angostura bitters
3 dashes orange bitters
3 dashes Peychaud's bitters
orange for garnish

Stir all the ingredients in a mixing glass filled with ice for 15 seconds. Strain into a rocks glass filled with ice and garnish with a flamed orange twist.

MARGOT TENENBAUM

D ram, the craft cocktail bar in the Williamsburg neighborhood of Brooklyn, opened in 2009 and helped popularize the bartender's choice, in which customers name their spirit and the bartender has the imaginative freedom to create a custom concoction. Nick Jarrett, who cited bourbon as his favorite spirit for the *Bartender Atlas* website, designed a family of drinks around the family members of the Wes Anderson movie *The Royal Tenenbaums*. While working alongside Jarrett at Dram, Frank Cisneros added this recipe to the family by taking a Gold Rush (page 119) and modifying it with Zucca, a deliciously bitter (just like Margot) Italian liqueur made from rhubarb. He chose Buffalo Trace because its rye content balances the honey nicely.

COUPE

2 ounces Buffalo Trace bourbon

½ ounce Zucca

¾ ounce lemon juice

½ ounce honey syrup (page 17)

Shake all the ingredients with ice and fine strain into a chilled coupe.

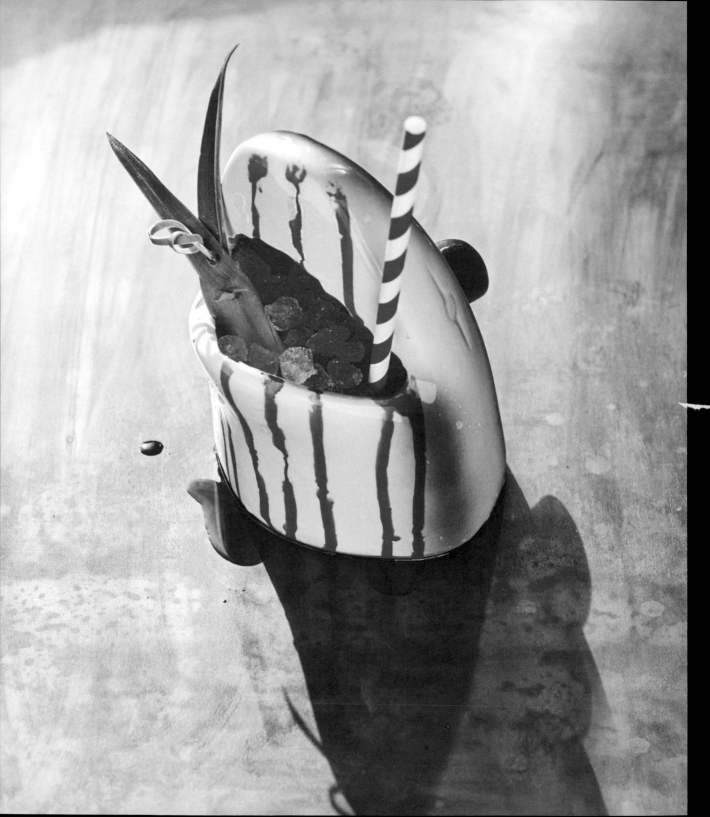

SHARK EYE

his cocktail takes bourbon on a spirited trip to the tropics. It draws inspiration from traditional tiki ingredients and combinations, but rather than the rum(s) you'd usually see, it makes use of more northerly spirits for its base. Cinnamon notes dominate the tiki bitters and add just the right amount of spice to the drink. Make it when you want a Zombie but are craving ~~brains~~ whiskey.

ROCKS

1½ ounce bourbon

½ ounce rye

¼ ounce dry Curaçao

¼ ounce maraschino liqueur

½ ounce passion fruit syrup

¾ ounce lemon juice

2 dashes Bittermens 'Elemakule Tiki bitters

pineapple fronds for garnish

Dry shake all the ingredients and pour into a shark mug filled with crushed ice. Drizzle the shark mouth with edible fake blood (see below). Garnish with pineapple frond mermaid tail and serve with a straw. If you don't have a shark cup—and every home bar needs at least one—use a rocks glass instead.

FAKE BLOOD

1½ ounces hot water

10 dashes Peychaud's bitters

10 drops red food coloring

1½ ounces white sugar

Mix all the ingredients until the sugar dissolves.

TEA ACT

The British Parliament passed the Tea Act in 1773 to reduce the amount of tea that the foundering British East India Company (EIC) owned and to discourage the smuggling of unlawful tea into the American colonies. The act required that colonists still pay import taxes on the EIC tea, though, which meant that Parliament was taxing Americans who had no representatives in Westminster. Smugglers and merchants formed an alliance to combat the new legislation, culminating in the Boston Tea Party in December 1773, which hastened the onset of the American War of Independence. Not long after, Basil Hayden, a Maryland farmer-distiller, relocated to Kentucky. His great-grandson opened the Old Grand Dad Distillery in 1882, named it in honor of his forefather, and put a portrait of his old (great) granddad on the label. The brand has changed hands many times, but it remains a prime whiskey. Its higher proof makes it easier to infuse with the smoky tea, and the tart, fruity gin, made with damson plums, tames those heavy smoke notes.

ROCKS

1 ounce Lapsang souchong–infused Old Grand Dad 114 bourbon

1 ounce Averell damson gin

¼ ounce Royal Combier

orange for garnish

Stir all the ingredients in a mixing glass filled with ice for 15 seconds. Strain into a rocks glass filled with ice. Garnish with an orange twist.

LAPSANG SOUCHONG–INFUSED OLD GRAND DAD

A little tea goes a long way, so tread carefully.

32 ounces Old Grand Dad 114 bourbon

1 ounce Lapsang souchong tea

Combine the ingredients and let sit for 30 minutes. Taste test. If you like the smoke level, strain out the tea. If you want more smokiness, continue infusing. The longer the tea steeps, the smokier and more tannic the bourbon will become.

UPSTATE LANDS

Brothers Todd and Scott Leopold grew up in Colorado and opened a brewery in Ann Arbor, Michigan, in 1999. Their success prompted them to grow the business to encompass spirits, which they began selling in 2001. They returned to the Centennial State in 2008 and set up shop in the Mile-High City. Leopold Bros. Distillery produces some great spirits, but one of the highlights of their collection and the centerpiece of this cocktail is their New York Sour Apple Liqueur. As they suggest, it's great for when you need acidity in a cocktail but not citrus or additional citrus notes. In this case, it makes for a refreshing fall cocktail. For the herb bouquet garnish, oregano, rosemary, sage, or thyme—or a combination thereof—will add savory notes and highlight the warmth of the bourbon.

ROCKS

1½ ounces Johnny Drum bourbon

¾ ounce Leopold Bros. New York Sour Apple Liqueur

½ ounce orange blossom simple syrup (see below)

½ ounce lemon juice

herb bouquet for garnish

Shake all the ingredients with ice and strain into a rocks glass filled with ice. Garnish with herb bouquet.

TIP

To make orange blossom simple syrup, steep an orange blossom tea bag in warm simple syrup (page 17) for 2 to 3 minutes.

THE RISE OF RYE

Around 2010, an obscene proliferation of flavored vodkas—bacon, cake, dill, grass, popcorn, salmon—hammered shut the coffin of vodka's cachet. Federal law designates vodka as colorless, odorless, and tasteless, but people were buying those abominations in ever-increasing numbers, which meant they didn't want vodka anymore. They wanted something warmer, something sweeter. They wanted whiskey. Pernod Ricard confirmed as much by releasing Oak by Absolut, a bourbon-flavored vodka, in September 2015, the exact time at which bourbon usurped the throne of national popularity.

Several years earlier, the Sazerac Company was rebranding Dr. McGillicuddy's Fireball Whisky, streamlining and relaunching it in 2007. As vodka foundered in oddball flavors, Fireball was flying off the shelves. But as vodka proved, when flavored versions of a spirit start proliferating, the cool factor is declining. Liquor stores now carry cinnamon, cherry, and apple whiskeys. Tastemakers—bartenders, chefs, editors, restaurateurs, and writers—aren't drinking those flavor bombs, though. They're turning to bourbon's spicier sibling, rye.

Rye isn't uniquely American, but American farmers, particularly in the North, have been converting it into alcohol for a long time. Here, then, is a short selection of whiskey cocktail recipes that call for rye as their base. If you don't have rye, you *can* substitute bourbon, but we don't recommend it. Four Roses Single Barrel has the highest rye content of any bourbon brand available nationally. Basil Hayden, Bulleit, and Old Grand Dad also have high-rye mash bills.

REMEMBER THE MAINE

In 1898, at the tail end of the Cuban War of Independence from Spain, President McKinley sent the USS *Maine* to monitor American interests in the Caribbean. The ship mysteriously exploded, and hundreds of American sailors died. Stateside newspapers, calling for war with Spain, bellowed the battle cry "Remember the *Maine*, to hell with Spain!" The recipe first appears in Charles Baker's *The Gentleman's Companion* (1939), in which he recalls drinking it during the Cuban Revolution of 1933. The drink bears a striking resemblance to the McKinley's Delight cocktail from Albert Stevens Crockett's *Old Waldorf-Astoria Bar Book* (1935).

COUPE

- 2 ounces rye
- ¾ ounce sweet vermouth
- ¼ ounce Cherry Heering
- 1 barspoon absinthe
  cocktail cherry for garnish

Stir all the liquid ingredients in a mixing glass filled with ice for 20 seconds and then strain into a chilled coupe. Garnish with a cherry.

SAZERAC

The Sazarac began life in New Orleans with Cognac as its base, specifically Sazerac de Forge et Fils. Tastes change, though, and by 1873 the brandy had become whiskey and absinthe had entered the mix. The cocktail evolved further when Sewell Taylor transferred his Merchants Exchange Coffee House to Aaron Bird in order to import Sazerac de Forge et Fils cognac. Bird changed the name of the establishment to Sazerac House and reengineered the house cocktail to include the bitters being made down the street by Antoine Peychaud and the Cognac that Taylor was importing.

ROCKS

1	dash absinthe
2	ounces rye
½	ounce demerara syrup (page 16)
2	dashes Peychaud's bitters
	lemon

Rinse a chilled rocks glass with absinthe. Stir the remaining ingredients in a mixing glass filled with ice for 15 seconds and then strain into the rocks glass. Expel oil from lemon twist over the top and discard.

VARIATION

Split the base 50–50 with rye and brandy or Cognac for even more delicious sipping.

VIEUX CARRÉ

Walter Bergeron invented this one—a little bit Sazerac, a little bit Manhattan, a little bit Saratoga—at the rotating Carousel Bar in the Hotel Monteleone in the French Quarter of New Orleans.

ROCKS

1	ounce brandy
1	ounce rye
1	ounce sweet vermouth
1	barspoon Bénédictine
2	dashes orange bitters
2	dashes Peychaud's bitters

Stir all the ingredients in a mixing glass filled with ice for 15 seconds and then strain into a rocks glass filled with ice. Garnish with a lemon twist.

OLD PAL

The Boulevardier and the Old Pal are brothers in cocktails. They go hand in hand, though this one tastes drier and crisper than its sibling. Harry MacElhone took inspiration from his old pal sports editor William "Sparrow" Robertson.

COUPE

1½	ounces Russell's Reserve rye
¾	ounce Campari
¾	ounce Dolin dry vermouth
	orange for garnish

Stir all the ingredients in a mixing glass filled with ice for 20 seconds, strain into a chilled coupe, and garnish with an orange twist.

THE BLINKER

The bitter sweetness of grapefruit juice gives us a lot of great cocktails. This one, from Patrick Gavin Duffy's *The Official Mixer's Manual* (1934), originally called for grenadine instead of raspberry syrup, but the syrup better complements the citrus tang of the grapefruit. Try it both ways to see which you prefer.

COUPE

1½	ounces rye
¼	ounce raspberry syrup
1	ounce grapefruit juice

Shake all the ingredients with ice and double strain into a chilled coupe.

BLEECKER

Anne Robinson created this riff on the Blinker in the summer of 2013 while bartending at PDT, New York City's most famous speakeasy, and named it for the street that runs from where the legendary punk rock club CBGB stood on the Bowery, through NYU and Greenwich Village, to the fashionable West Village.

COUPE

2	ounces Bulleit rye
½	ounce lemon juice
⅓	ounce Zucca
1	teaspoon Bonne Maman raspberry preserves
1	dash Bittermens Xocolatl Mole bitters
	lemon for garnish

Shake all the ingredients with ice and fine strain into a chilled coupe. Garnish with lemon wheel.

SOUND OF SILVER

Music inspired this cocktail named for the LCD Soundsystem album playing during its invention. Velvet Falernum—a mixture of lime, cloves, ginger, and almond—sweetens and gives body to split-base, Old-Fashioned–style drinks like this one.

ROCKS

1	ounce apple brandy
1	ounce Rittenhouse rye
½	ounce Velvet Falernum
¼	ounce Gran Classico
2	dashes rosemary tincture
	lime for garnish

Stir all the ingredients in a mixing glass filled with ice for 15 seconds and then strain into a rocks glass filled with ice. Garnish with a lime twist.

BARS, FESTIVALS, READING, GLOSSARY & INDEXES

THE BEST BOURBON BARS

CALIFORNIA
Acme Bar & Company, Berkeley,
  acmebarandcompany.com

Bourbon and Branch, San Francisco,
  bourbonandbranch.com

Rickhouse, San Francisco, *rickhousebar.com*

COLORADO
Bull & Bush, Denver, *bullandbush.com*

The Whiskey, Ft. Collins, *thewhiskeyfc.com*

DISTRICT OF COLUMBIA
Jack Rose Dining Saloon, *jackrosediningsaloon.com*

ILLINOIS
Big Star, Chicago, *bigstarchicago.com*

Delilah's, Chicago, *delilahschicago.com*

KENTUCKY
Bluegrass Tavern, Lexington, *thebluegrasstavern.com*

Bourbons Bistro, Louisville, *bourbonsbistro.com*

Charr'd Bourbon Kitchen and Lounge, Louisville,
  *marriott.com/hotel-restaurants/sdfls-louisville-
  marriott-east/carrd-bourbon-kitchen-and-
  lounge/5303541/home-page.mi*

Doc Crows, Louisville, *doccrows.com*

Down One Bourbon Bar, Louisville,
  downonebourbonbar.com

Haymarket Whiskey Bar, Louisville,
  haymarketwhiskeybar.com

The Old Talbott Tavern, Bardstown, *talbotts.com*

The Paddock Bar and Patio, Lexington, *no web address*

Proof on Main, Louisville, *proofonmain.com*

The Rickhouse, Bardstown,
  therickhouse-bardstown.com

The Silver Dollar, Louisville, *whiskeybythedrink.com*

MICHIGAN
Butter Run Saloon, St. Clair Shores, *butterrun.com*

MINNESOTA
Butcher & the Boar, Minneapolis,
  butcherandtheboar.com

NEW YORK
Al's Wine & Whiskey Lounge, Syracuse,
  alswineandwhiskey.com

Beast of Bourbon, Brooklyn, *beastofbourbonbk.com*

Brandy Library, New York City, *brandylibrary.com*

The Flatiron Room, New York City, *theflatironroom.com*

Maysville, New York City, *maysvillenyc.com*

Noorman's Kil, Brooklyn, *noormanskil.com*

Post Office, Brooklyn, *postofficebk.com*

OREGON
Multnomah Whiskey Library, Portland, *mwlpdx.com*

SOUTH CAROLINA
Husk, Charleston, *huskrestaurant.com*

TENNESSEE
Patterson House, Nashville, *thepattersonnashville.com*

Whiskey Kitchen, Nashville,
  mstreetnashville.com/whiskey-kitchen

TEXAS
Julep, Houston, *julephouston.com*

The Standard Pour, Dallas, *tspdallas.com*

WASHINGTON
Canon, Seattle, *canonseattle.com*

FESTIVALS & EVENTS

BEER, BOURBON & BBQ FESTIVAL
Locations vary
BeerAndBourbon.com

BOURBON AND BEYOND
Louisville, Kentucky
BourbonAndBeyond.com

KENTUCKY BOURBON AFFAIR
Louisville, Kentucky
KYBourbonAffair.com

KENTUCKY BOURBON FESTIVAL
Bardstown, Kentucky
KYBourbonFestival.com

NEW ORLEANS BOURBON FESTIVAL
New Orleans, Louisiana
NewOrleansBourbonFestival.com

SUN WHISKEY UNION
Uncasville, Connecticut
MoheganSun.com/sun-whiskey-union.html

UNIVERSAL WHISKEY EXPERIENCE
Las Vegas, Nevada
UniversalWhiskyExperience.com

WHISKEY ON ICE
Minneapolis, Minnesota
WhiskeyOnIceMN.com

WHISKIES OF THE WORLD
Locations vary
WhiskiesOfTheWorld.com

FURTHER READING

American Whiskey, Bourbon & Rye by Clay Risen

The Book of Bourbon and Other Fine American Whiskeys by Gary Regan and Mardee Haidin Regan

Bourbon by Fred Minnick

Bourbon Curious by Fred Minnick

Bourbon Empire by Reid Mitenbuler

Bourbon in Kentucky by Chester Zoeller

Bourbon Whiskey, Our Native Spirit by Bernie Lubbers

Bourbon, Straight by Charles Cowdery

Bourbon, Strange by Charles Cowdery

But Always Fine Bourbon by Sally van Winkle Campbell

Kentucky Bourbon Barons by Chester Zoeller

Kentucky Bourbon Country by Susan Reigler

Kentucky Bourbon Whiskey by Michael Veach

The Manhattan by Philip Greene

Potions of the Caribbean by Jeff Berry

Proof by Adam Rogers

Straight Up or on the Rocks by William Grimes

Tasting Whiskey by Lew Bryson

The Curious Bartender: An Odyssey of Malt, Bourbon & Rye Whiskies by Tristan Stephenson

The Old-Fashioned by Robert Simonson

Whiskey. The Definitive World Guide by Michael Jackson

Whiskey Women by Fred Minnick

The World Atlas of Whiskey by Dave Broom

IMAGE CREDITS

GLOSSARY OF SELECT TERMS

ALCOHOL AND TOBACCO TAX AND TRADE BUREAU Commonly referred to as the acronym TTB, this federal bureau regulates the production of alcohol, maintaining specific rules for production, labeling, and distribution. These rules include guidelines for determining what can or cannot be called bourbon or whiskey.

BARREL-AGING Storage of distilled spirits in a wooden barrel. The wood absorbs impurities from the liquor while imparting certain color, aroma, and flavor. All categories of whiskey (except corn whiskey) must be stored in a barrel. American whiskeys in general don't have a minimum age limit, although straight bourbon must age for at least two years.

BOTTLED IN BOND The bourbon was made at a single distillery, by one distiller, in one distillation season. It aged for at least four years in a federally bonded and supervised warehouse and was bottled at 100 proof.

BOURBON Whiskey produced in the U.S. at not exceeding 80 percent alcohol by volume (160 proof) from a fermented mash of not less than 51 percent corn and stored at not more than 62.5 percent alcohol by volume (125 proof) in charred new oak containers.

CASK STRENGTH Bottled directly from the barrel with no water added to adjust the proof.

CHAR The level at which the inside of a barrel is burned. A char number denotes the amount of time for which the wood is exposed to the flame. Number 1 is 15 seconds, 2 is 30, 3 is 35, and 4, the most common, is 55 seconds. Number 4 is called "alligator char" because the interior of the staves resemble the rough, shiny texture of alligator skin.

CORN WHISKEY Similar to bourbon but different. The mash bill of this corn-based spirit must consist of at least 80 percent corn (unlike bourbon's 51 percent). It cannot come off the still any higher than 160 proof. Legally it doesn't need aging, but, if it is aged, it must do so in oak barrels at no more than 125 proof.

EDUCATED GLASS A glass from which whiskey has been sipped already. The residual notes from the spirit linger in the glass and enchance the next serving of the same whiskey.

MASH The mixture of cooked grains and water before the distiller adds yeast to start fermentation.

MASHBILL The grain recipe used to make whiskey, for example:

Corn 51%	Corn 60%	Corn 75%
Wheat 45%	Rye 36%	Rye 21%
Barley Malt 4%	Barley Malt 4%	Barley Malt: 4%

SINGLE BARREL All of the whiskey in this line comes from one barrel. Distillers often blend whiskey to adhere to the brand's flavor profile. For a single barrel, the distiller chooses one exceptional barrel for bottling, thereby showcasing his or her skills more clearly.

SMALL BATCH A limited number of barrels blended together.

STRAIGHT BOURBON WHISKEY Bourbon whiskey stored in charred new oak containers for two years or more. It may include mixtures of two or more straight bourbon whiskeys provided all of the whiskeys are produced in the same state.

TENNESSEE WHISKEY Not the same as bourbon! All Tennessee whiskey must come from Tennessee, but bourbon can come from any state in the Union. Both contain mostly corn, and both age in new American oak. With one distillery exception, all Tennessee whiskey uses the Lincoln County Process, which includes charcoal filtration before barrel aging.

WHISKEY Spirits distilled from a fermented mash of grain at less than 95 percent alcohol by volume (190 proof) having the taste, aroma, and characteristics generally attributed to whiskey and bottled at not less than 40 percent alcohol by volume (80 proof).

RECIPE & INGREDIENT INDEX

GENERAL INDEX

ABOUT THE AUTHORS

JANE DANGER is coauthor of *Cuban Cocktails* (Sterling Epicure) and began her bartending career at CBGB before moving to Death & Co., PDT, and NoMad Bar. She consults on and contributes to cocktail menus all along the East Coast, and her work has appeared in *Food and Wine, Imbibe, New York* magazine, *Time Out New York, New York Post*, the *New York Times, The PDT Cocktail Book*, and *Mr. Boston 75th Anniversary Guide*. She lives in New York City.

ALLA LAPUSHCHIK is coauthor of *Cuban Cocktails* (Sterling Epicure). She assisted with the opening of the Bourgeois Pig before moving to Death & Co. and other bars. After opening Post Office in South Williamsburg,

she also opened OTB, which focuses on craft spirits and comfort food. *Time Out New York* included her among "Brooklyn's New Order," and she has been featured in *Brooklyn Spirits* by Peter Thomas Fontanale and Chris Wertz, *Imbibe* magazine, *The New York Times*, and *Village Voice*. She lives in Brooklyn.

CLAY RISEN is a senior editor at the *New York Times* and the drinks columnist for *Garden & Gun*. He has written for *The Atlantic, Fortune, Smithsonian*, and the *Washington Post* and is the author of *American Whiskey, Bourbon & Rye* (Sterling Epicure). He lives in Brooklyn with his wife and two young children.